MY IDENTITY IS IN CHRIST

DISCOVERING THE FREEDOM
GOD ALWAYS INTENDED

BONNIE WOODS O'NEIL

My Identity is in Christ

I dedicate this book to my wonderful parents,
Dolly and Bill Woods,
who first taught me of the Father's deep love for me,
and who demonstrated
that even in the deepest of personal tragedies,
the safest place to be
is resting securely in Father's arms.
With deep love and gratitude.

Table of Contents

Introduction	"You'll Come" Hillsong United - "The I Heart Revolution" (Live)
1. The Proverbs 31 Woman	"Everything" Tim Hughes – "Holding Nothing Back"
2. Hannah	"Love is Here" Tenth Avenue North – "Over and Underneath"
3. Rebekah	"Lead Me to the Cross" Hillsong United – "All of the Above"
4. Leah	"Beautiful Things" Gungor – "Beautiful Things"
5. Eve	"Hungry (Falling on My Knees)" Joy Williams – "WOW Worship"
6. Sapphira	"My Desire" Jeremy Camp – "Restored"
7. Sarah and the Woman with the Hemorrhage	"Healer" Hillsong Live – "This is Our God"
8. Rahab	"Amazing Grace (My Chains Are Gone)" Chris Tomlin – "How Great is Our God"
9. Breaking Free	"Break Every Chain" Jesus Culture – "Awakening - Live from Chicago"
10. Staying Free	"Rooftops" Jesus Culture – "Come Away (Live)"

Introduction

Like many projects that God calls us to undertake, this Bible study began with a cry of my heart. I yearned for the women in my Bible study—most of whom were young in their faith—to know God more fully. It was clear that they wanted to know God in a deeper way, yet many of them were not comfortable opening up the Word of God by themselves and trying to get to know Him on their own. The Bible seemed like a book of deep mysteries too difficult to decipher on their own. Where does one even begin to try to understand this vast book? So in my prayers for these women, I kept asking God to give them a love for His word and to stop them from being too intimidated to open His Word on their own. I was thinking about Bible studies that would be appropriate for them, something that would touch the heart of these women by speaking into their longings, as well as encourage them to open up the Word for themselves.

After months of prayer for my friends and for their desire to read the Word of God themselves, the Lord—as only He can do—gave me nearly the entire framework for this Bible study in one full shot as I was driving home from Philadelphia on the Schuylkill Expressway. Were it not for the bumper-to-bumper traffic that brought my fellow travelers and me to a standstill, I would have needed to pull over to the side of the road to scratch out the details of what He was showing me. While God was clear and decisive in giving me the outline for this book, I was less quick to respond in writing it. It has taken me several years of not believing that I was either capable or called to write this book, and many years of finding other things to do to occupy my time before He grabbed hold of me and enabled me to finish it wholeheartedly. Our fledgling little Bible study has long since broken up as many of my friends have moved not just out of state but out of the country as well. But wherever God leads you Nancy, Judy, Margie, Marita, Joan, Tami, and Kate, this study is for you, and for anyone else who wants to know God more richly and to see what He has to say to you personally through His Word.

I live in the western suburbs of Philadelphia, referred to as the Philadelphia Main Line, because the towns in this area were built along the old Main Line of the Philadelphia Railroad. This is the land of "old money", where Philadelphia's wealthiest families in the 19th century built their country estates. Places like this are where the expression "keeping up with the Joneses" must have originated! Competition to succeed and appear to have it all is tremendous. Because of the competitive nature of the area in which I currently live, it seems as though women around here struggle all the more with questions of their own identity: who am I in terms of my career, my physical and athletic abilities, my wealth, my status within the community, my physical appearance, my children's success, and so forth. It has been obvious to me for years that these are issues that we women struggle with, particularly in the area in which I live. Perhaps you would not describe where you live as being anything like Main Line Philadelphia, but I believe these struggles are common to all women and that God has graciously given us examples in His Word of women who wrestled with these very same things. Some of the women we will look at together relied on Him for their true sense of identity, and others did not; all of them have much to teach us about forming our identity in God alone.

In our culture, it seems the moment we are born we enter into a race for personal achievement and success. The rules of the game are very strict, are known by all, and are shouted at us constantly, beginning with our parents and continuing with our teachers, bosses, and the greater community. "Do this, and you will be accepted." "Try this, and you will be more beautiful." "Say this, and you will never be found at fault." "Do that, and your children will get ahead." The messages to get ahead are everywhere and they all lead to the same place—DESPAIR. Despair that we have to keep doing more or we won't be good enough. Despair that we might *never* measure up.

The Lord is the answer to all of our needs. We may know Him as Savior and trust in Him to provide, yet often we allow other concerns to prevent us from relying solely on Him. We have many perceived needs—of acceptance, status, beauty, success in our children, success in our careers—that get in the way of relying solely on the Lord God and in finding our identity in Him alone. We strive to find our satisfaction in so many things, but ultimately, God alone will satisfy our deepest longings. It is my prayer that through this study we would be able to come to His scripture with confidence knowing that therein we will find the answers to all of our questions about who we are and how our identity can be formed in God and in God alone.

We will be looking together at women in the Bible who struggled with many of these same identity issues. As you read the passages for each chapter, please pay particular attention to the central woman. Imagine what she was like. Learn about her. Allow her to come to life for you. Imagine her relationship with God and with her family. Can you see yourself in her? How are you similar? How are you different? Where has she placed her identity? Do you sometimes put your identity in the same things as she does?

This Bible study is intended to help us identify areas of bondage where we have placed our identity in something other than in the Lord Jesus Christ, and is also meant to be a means by which we can grow in Bible literacy. It has been my prayer that in going through this study you would not only learn where your own strongholds are, but that you would also grow in your comfort level in reading the Bible and in digging into the scriptures to see how the Lord wants to speak to you.

As you read these chapters, please do so not only with the book in your hand, but with your Bible by your side as well. I will give a main scripture passage that accompanies each chapter. Please read the verses before you begin reading the material and take the time to look up each additional verse that is referenced in the chapter. If any of these supplemental verses inspires you, keep reading! God can do some of His best work in us when we explore scripture and see where He wants to take us. Please take the time to write your answers in this book as though it were a journal-don't just think about it-write it out, taking your time to see what the Lord is teaching you.

Bible study is meant to show us where our hearts are far from God and where we are relying on our own strength rather than on His power working through us. It is meant ultimately to lead us to a time of worship and praise, and so I have compiled a collection of worship songs that accompany each chapter that I hope you will be able to access on-line. My prayer is that the song associated with each lesson will help you in your time of praise and adoration of our Lord. Allow God to speak into your heart how He desires to transform you into the image of His Son where your identity is fully grounded in the Lord Jesus Christ.

As you begin this study, please listen to "You'll Come" by Hillsong United on "The I Heart Revolution (Live)" album. As you commit yourself to waiting upon the Lord and learning from Him, be assured that He will come to you. Give Him your thirsty heart and let Him flood your soul. Open your heart to Him and He will come.

1

The Proverbs 31 Woman
Proverbs 31: 10-31

What does "My Identity is in Christ" mean? What exactly is an "identity"? Webster's Dictionary says that an identity is "the distinguishing character or personality of an individual; the relation established by psychological identification."[1] Clearly, things we identify with can have deep psychological roots and can stem from past experiences, fears, pleasures, and inborn personality traits. God tells us right from the beginning of His word to us in Genesis that we were made in His image and as such He wants us to rely on Him and find our identity in Him. The Psalmist David describes our reliance on God this way, "For You are my rock and fortress; for Your name's sake You will lead me and guide me...for You are my strength." (Psalms 31: 3-4, ESV)

What would my life look like if my distinguishing character were Christ? What if my personality were that of Christ? What if on the deepest psychological level others saw Christ in me and not the dysfunctional behavior I carry around? What would that look like?

When under pressure, what character traits do others see in you?

What do you wish people would see in you?

Let's look together at perhaps the most hated woman in the whole Bible: the Proverbs 31 Woman. She seems to do everything right! Read the passage and list as many adjectives, phrases, and characteristic traits about her as you can. Please take the time to be thorough here; the list is extensive!

This woman's list of attributes is truly remarkable. If you wrote down everything you observed, your list might look something like this: virtuous, capable, trustworthy, helper, industrious, busy, curious, creative, likes international cuisine, an early riser, giving, serving, organized, manager, decision-maker, business woman, manages finances, energetic, strong, works hard, thrifty, works late into the night, good at handcrafts, has a cottage business, helps the poor, generous, prepares in advance, dresses well, enriches her husband's life, is skilled at farming, sewing, and finance, physically fit, strong of character, dignified, embraces the future, fearless, wise, does not worry, kind, speaks only and always with wisdom and kindness, strong domestic manager, would never entertain laziness, her children respect and praise her, her husband praises her, she's the top of the top, she fears-meaning she honors, loves and respects-the Lord. Whew! What a list of attributes!

Before you rip this entire chapter out of your Bibles, let me say a few words about the Book of Proverbs. First, Proverbs is a book of Poetry meant to instruct the reader in true wisdom. In Proverbs, "the wise man" is the one who is choosing to live by God's standards, while "the fool" is the one who is making his own choices of right and wrong behavior. Throughout Proverbs, many idealized examples of wise men are given with very little said about women other than in chapters 1, 8, and 9, where we see Wisdom personified as a woman. In these chapters she gives instruction to her, most likely, male students and listeners. This language doesn't lead the reader to envision a *real* woman, but rather a divinely sanctioned spokesperson of Wisdom. Finally, at the end of the book, a beautiful example of a flesh and blood wise woman is given, reminding us how much God cares about and is not prejudiced against women.

Secondly, this wisdom poem is an acrostic, in which each verse begins with the successive letter of the 22 letters of the Hebrew alphabet. The poem begins and ends with mention of the woman's excellence. The probable intention of putting this together with the acrostic pattern is to show that this woman's character runs the whole range of excellence.[2] This is an ideal; no one woman could possibly excel in *all* these areas! But perhaps you can find *some* elements of yourself in here, and identify others that God is nudging you to work on. What I like about her is that she has developed a keen sense of who she is physically, mentally, and spiritually; she is devoted to the wellbeing of her household—her husband and children—and manages well their internal domestic affairs; and she has some active engagement in external economic concerns.

Identify a few attributes of this woman that are true of you as well. Do you cook well for your family? Do you actively seek to strengthen your body and be healthy? Do you plan ahead to keep your busy family organized?

Are you well-skilled at your profession? Are you a conscientious manager of your employees and family members?

In terms of *outward accomplishments*, in what ways does this woman seem to resemble the typical Modern Over-Achieving Woman? What makes her different?

So she's put together and on her A-game, but does that necessarily mean she draws her strength for all her amazing accomplishments from God? How do we know she isn't simply the poster child of the Modern Over-Achieving Woman? Verse 30 gives us great insight into the source of her strength.

Reread verse 30. What is the anchor in this woman's life?

She is a woman "who fears the Lord." "The fear of the LORD" is a wonderful phrase used throughout scripture, indicating a response of reverence, awe, and humility before our Maker and Redeemer. It is not a casual sentiment but a deeply rooted reverence for God that leads one to want to please Him. In other words, it is a belief that leads to action. One who fears the Lord will by definition *look* different and *act* differently from someone who does not fear the Lord. Proverbs 1:7 states that "the fear of the LORD is the beginning of knowledge". When we have a response of reverence, awe and humility before the Lord, He will be able to fill us with true wisdom and understanding. When we respond to situations with wisdom rather than folly, we will begin to see our identity changed to being the identity of Christ. The Proverbs 31 Woman places her identity in the Lord and as a result does not struggle with the same identity issues as do the women whose lives we will be examining in subsequent chapters.

Unlike Hannah, who has to learn to give God total control over her work, the Proverbs 31 Woman does not place her identity in her work. It is clear from the text that she has a thriving business or two in addition to the nurture and support she gives to her husband and children. She is into real estate, agriculture, and fashion design and production. She is eager to get started every morning and is in no rush to call it quits before day's end. And yet, you don't get the sense that she is a bundle of nerves trying to accomplish all that the day has for her! I think we all know women like that (perhaps you are one of them!) and it would not be said of them that when they speak, they only have kind things to say (verse 26). People under pressure are all too apt to explode to let off steam! Whether at home or in one of her businesses, "she senses the worth of her work" (verse 18 MSG) and that is the key to her avoiding placing her identity in her work. She knows her work is worthwhile in itself; she doesn't do it to provide herself with a sense of worth.

The 22 verses that describe the Proverbs 31 Woman don't give a description of her physical appearance as do the verses about Leah. We don't know if she was a beauty, but the writer's assessment in verse 30 that "beauty is vain" (NAS) or "beauty soon fades" (MSG) gives us an indication of how little this woman depends on beauty for her sense of identity and worth. Maybe she wasn't a beauty, but nevertheless she took good care of herself and took the time to look elegant. One can look elegant and pulled together without being a beauty! It can be a challenge especially in today's world of cosmetic enhancements to take good care of our appearance without becoming obsessed with our own image, but this woman gives us the secret. She knows, and undoubtedly reminds herself, that beauty is vain, and she "smiles at the future" (verse 25)—wrinkles, gray hair, achy bones, and all!

We will examine the life of Rebekkah, who, along with her husband, Isaac, and their son Jacob, will struggle with placing her identity in one of her children. Our Proverbs 31 Woman keeps all of her children busy and productive and clearly has no favorites among them. Her children respect and praise her. I wonder if deep down Jacob really *respected* his mother Rebekkah? A woman whose ultimate respect and admiration is directed toward the Lord cannot be found placing her identity in her children.

The first woman we meet in the Bible, Eve, will struggle with a common identity issue: the need to always be right. The Proverbs 31 Woman does not struggle with this stronghold. She is very careful with her words, never speaking spitefully, and always speaking with wisdom and kindness. We know she is not worried about exalting herself because her husband trusts her without reserve (verse 11, MSG) and her children rise up and bless her (verse 28, NAS). A need to always be right will not engender complete trust and words of blessing from those in our immediate family! When was the last time your children stood up and praised you after you spoke unkindly to them?

One of our New Testament women, Sapphira, will place all of her identity in her popularity within her local community as she strives to get ahead. The Proverbs 31 Woman is highly respected within her community without ever seeming to fret about her status. She is a successful businesswoman, a generous philanthropist, and speaks only with kindness and wisdom. She is a woman of integrity, and unlike Sapphira, is not one to be swayed by dishonesty in order to get ahead. You get the sense that her husband is actually *more* highly regarded *because* of her. In a chapter all about the excellent wife, two anchoring verses—one at the beginning (verse 11) and one near the end (verse 23)—interrupt us with words about her husband. First we learn that he trusts her, and then we learn that he himself is greatly respected within the community. The placement of these two verses in this way leads the reader to see the causal relationship between his trust in her, and his position of respect within the community. Because he can trust her so implicitly, he is free to go about his work in strength and confidence. The excellent wife and her husband enjoy the respect of their community in part because the motivation for their actions is not to become more popular; they work, they serve, and they give because they know the inherent worth of these activities.

Not much is written about the health of the Proverbs 31 Woman. We do know that she has tremendous energy to accomplish all that she does in a day, especially considering that she rises early and works late into the evening! We will compare the lives of two women, Sarah in the Old Testament, and the woman with the hemorrhage in the New Testament, to see how they dealt with their own health concerns. Whether the Proverbs 31 Woman is healthy or not, her fear of the Lord, her commitment not to "eat the bread of idleness" (verse 27), and her lack of fear about the future point to a woman who has not placed her identity in her health.

Everyone has baggage from their past—the painful experiences that we wish never happened and that we just can't seem to shake. Unlike Rahab, whose life as a prostitute is detailed in the book of Joshua, we don't know what past experiences the Proverbs 31 Woman carries around with her. But we can be sure she has some; we all do! The question regarding our past baggage is whether or not we let it define us. Whatever may have happened in this woman's past, she finds her present work to be worthy, she has no fear of the future, and she most certainly has placed her identity in the Lord.

With so much going on in this busy woman's life, how does she keep her eyes focused on God and find her strength in Him and not in herself or other things? She begins by ensuring that her life reflects godly qualities, then she diligently builds a strong and healthy domestic life, both of which enable her to go forward in confidence in her professional and vocational activities. We will examine each of these three components of her life in turn.

HER GODLY CHARACTER

We learn a lot about this woman in a few short verses. Many of her characteristic traits focus on her inner character. She is virtuous, trustworthy, curious, creative, giving, energetic, strong, generous, strong of character, dignified, fearless, wise, kind, and she speaks only and always with wisdom and kindness. While no one person can ever display *all* of these traits 24/7, clearly God is giving us a goal to strive to meet. How does one even begin to be fearless and wise, curious and trustworthy, energetic and kind all at the same time? Her starting point is that she fears—meaning she honors, loves and respects—the Lord.

When our love, honor, and respect for God are the primary motivators in our lives, our lives will look different from those around us. When our eyes are focused on God and not ourselves, we can be kindhearted to others without fear of being taken advantage of. When our significance comes from God alone, we will be trustworthy individuals, for nothing will be added to our self-worth if we are found knowing things others don't yet know. When we trust wholeheartedly in God, our creativity and our energy will be blessed by Him and used for His kingdom's work. When our sense of worth is rooted in God alone, we will live generous lives, not fearing whether our own needs, real or imagined, will be met.

Long before the giving of the Holy Spirit at Pentecost, this woman lives her life as though she is filled with the Holy Spirit of God. She lives every day with the sense that her body is the temple of the Holy Spirit and as such, she lives to be pleasing to her God. Since Pentecost, each of us who has accepted Christ as lord of our lives has been sealed and filled with the Holy Spirit. The work we do of forming godly character we do not do alone. He has given us His Spirit as a Helper in this process of transformation.

How do you personally rely on the Holy Spirit's work in transforming you, rather than expending lots of effort to change on your own?

Of all the phrases that describe this woman's godly character, one of the phrases that strikes me the most is that "she speaks only and always with wisdom and kindness." James tells us that the mouth is the most difficult part of the body to control. He goes so far as to say that "no one can tame the tongue." (James 3:8) If we want to develop godly *inner* qualities, a great place to begin is to practice speaking with a *godly* tongue. If you are anything like me, you might wonder how in the world we begin to tame these tongues of ours.

In his letter to the church at Philippi, Paul gives us this insight—be careful what goes in if you want to control want comes out! He says in Philippians 4:8 "Whatever is true, whatever is honorable, whatever is right, whatever is pure, whatever is lovely, whatever is of good repute, if there is any excellence and if anything worthy of praise, let your mind dwell on these things." When we train our minds to dwell on the good we see, it will be a starting point to training our lips to speak kind words.

What might this look like in practice? Picture that thing your husband does that always annoys you. What do you tend to do about it? If you're like me, your eye becomes like a telescope as you focus in on that one thing, again, and again, and again. And then, before we even know that our lips are moving, we have allowed the grumble to pass our lips! Subconsciously we think that if we just express ourselves this one last time, we will finally be understood and we will get our way! Ladies, we have a bad, deserved reputation as nags! The writer of Proverbs even compares our incessant nagging to the sound of a dripping faucet! (Isn't that what is used in some forms of military torture?) "A nagging spouse is like the drip, drip, drip of a leaky faucet" (MSG Prov 27:15)

If we follow Paul's teaching, we would refuse to allow our eye to telescope in on the *one* thing that annoys us and would instead focus our eye and thoughts on the *many* things they do that are true, honorable, right, pure, lovely, of good repute, excellent, or worthy of praise. That's a long list of attributes; surely there is much from that list that we could train our minds to focus on instead of the one thing (or two or three things) that will inevitably cause us to grumble. When we train our thoughts to center on what's right instead of what's wrong, we will be on our way to training our mouths to speak what is wise and kind.

In order to grow in wisdom and kindness, our Proverbs 31 Woman makes a practice of only speaking words that are wise and kind. It is clear that part of her plan in forming godly character involves intentionally practicing those very character traits she wants to develop.

Have you ever made a commitment to speak only words that were wise and kind? How often do you make a concerted effort to choose a kind word over a quick retort?

_____

How can you speak only what is worthwhile and speak with wisdom and kindness when you are in a disagreement with your husband or when you are disciplining one of your children? What might this look like?

_____

Is there an area of your inner character that you sense God wants you to trust Him with? Your choice of words? Your creativity? Your energy or strength? The things you can give away to others? Your fears? Offer it to Him now as a prayer of commitment.

HER STRONG AND HEALTHY DOMESTIC LIFE

Many of her character traits are what enable her to have a strong and healthy domestic life. I think we would all say we wanted a strong and healthy home life, but are we willing to do the work involved in building these characteristics? Words that describe how she functions in her domestic setting are: a helper, busy, strong domestic manager, likes international cuisine, an early riser, practiced at serving others, organized, thrifty, good at handcrafts, works late into the night, helps the poor, prepares in advance, dresses well, enriches her husband's life, and embraces the future. Because of the strength of her character, her husband and her children respect and praise her.

Our Proverbs 31 Woman does more than just develop godly character; she actively builds a strong and healthy domestic life, beginning with her relationship with her husband and extending to her relationships with her children. The very first thing that is mentioned in the long list of accolades about her is that "she does (her husband) good and not evil all the days of her life." (Verse 12) It is very easy for us to read through that verse quickly and conclude, "I have that covered; I don't do anything evil to my husband." But the Message version casts a slightly larger vision of "evil" and states: "never spiteful, she treats him generously all her life long."

Always generous…never spiteful? Ouch! How difficult is that for us? We ladies can be so prone to getting our feelings hurt, especially from our men, and our responses to them can often be quite spiteful in return.

When your husband makes a comment that hurts your feelings, do you want to strike back with a sharp, spiteful comment or can you calmly address the matter with him?

_____

Proverbs 21:9 tells us "it is better to live in the corner of a roof than in a house shared with a contentious woman." We can be so argumentative, can't we? Our sense of who we are should not crumble from one negative word; rather, we should be able to stand firm in the love of the Father for us. When our identity is firmly rooted in God, a sharp word from a loved one will not have a disastrous effect on our self-esteem and should not produce in us a string of venomous words in response.

In your own life, how difficult is it for you to guard your tongue when a member of your family, a dear friend, or a co-worker says something that upsets you?

_____

How about your attitudes with your children? When they act like whiny young children or mouthy teenagers, do you respond to them spitefully or with firm grace?

_____

Proverbs 13:3 cautions us that "the one who guards his mouth preserves his life" and Proverbs 14:1 tells us that "the wise woman builds up her house while the foolish woman tears it down with her own hands."

How careful are you to avoid cynicism within your family? If you removed all cynicism from your speech, would you have much left to say?

When the fear of the Lord anchors us at the deepest levels, we will allow Him to transform us so that we will desire to help and serve our families, even when it is easier to serve ourselves. Do you believe He will supply you with the energy to give of yourself to those He has entrusted to your care, even when you don't feel like it? Believe it! The Proverbs 31 Woman sets a beautiful example of rising early—as a gift to her family—to make them breakfast and send them off *well* for their day at work or school. Women truly are the gatekeepers of the emotions in a home; take advantage of these first moments in the day before everyone disperses, and make the time sweet. Even when the hour is too early for us to *feel* sweet, *be* sweet, as you send them off.

When we dedicate the work of our hands to the Lord, asking Him to fill us with curiosity and creativity, even the meals we prepare for our families can take on a whole new flavor. With a world full of internet recipes at your disposal, you no longer have to go to far away places to bring the exotic to your home! Our gifts of time and creativity may not be appreciated by everyone in the family, every day of the week, but on the whole, they contribute to the emotional strength and fabric of the home.

When our kindness and wisdom grow out of our love for God, we will also be able to help the poor and embrace the future without fear. When we have learned to speak only and always with wisdom and kindness, we will no longer engage in patterns of spiteful, cynical comments to the ones we love. When we allow the fear of the Lord to shape our view of ourselves, our godly character will help us build a strong and healthy home life where our husbands and children honor and respect us.

HER PROFESSIONAL AND VOCATIONAL ACTIVITIES

Like the Proverbs 31 Woman, once we are growing in godly character, and we are fostering healthy relationships within our immediate family, then we will be in a position to flourish in our professional and vocational activities. Transformation always begins within—with our relationship with God—and then works itself outward, first with our families and then with other people and activities. Words that describe this woman's professional life are: capable, industrious, manager, decision-maker, businesswoman, manager of finances, hard worker, is skilled at farming, sewing, and finance, embraces the future, and would never entertain laziness.

There is no distinction between domestic and professional work in God's eyes. Did you notice that the Proverbs 31 woman works hard at home even though she has servants (maidens)? She is diligent in homemaking, even though she is a successful businesswoman, and has others who could do the domestic work for her. Does homemaking ever seem unimportant to you? Does it seem like a less valuable occupation than a big job with a big paycheck? Don't get caught in the trap of thinking that homemaking is not a worthwhile pursuit. This modern cultural mindset and is not what God expresses in Proverbs 31. We sense the success of the Proverbs 31 family is largely due to what *she* puts into it. What she does in the home enables the other family members to do their work with excellence and in confidence.

There is also no distinction between God's work and secular work. All of our work is meant to bring glory to God and to His kingdom. Paul reminds us in 1 Corinthians 10:31, "whatever you do, do all to the glory of

26

God." We have all been given work to do and we are all called to work as unto God, not man. When our identity is in God, our work itself can be an offering to Him.

Immediately following his passage on the fruit of the Spirit in a believer who is growing in Christlikeness, Paul offers us these words about our life and work: "Live creatively, friends...Make a careful exploration of who you are and the work you have been given, and then sink yourself into that. Don't be impressed with yourself. Don't compare yourself with others. Each of you must take responsibility for doing the creative best you can with your own life." (Galatians 6:1, 4-5 MSG)

How can you make the work that you have been given an offering to God?

How can we live like the Proverbs 31 Woman? How do we ensure that our identity is in Christ and not in the myriad other things that vie for our attention? Like the Proverbs 31 Woman, we must begin by developing a deep fear of the Lord, which as we read in Proverbs 1:7 is where true wisdom begins. Proverbs 2:3-7 tells us that we must diligently seek to grow in wisdom, discernment, and understanding, and continues in the following chapter by reminding us that the rewards of knowing the fear and wisdom of the Lord are great.

Read Proverbs 3:1-35 and list as many benefits of gaining godly wisdom as you can. Here again, don't rush through this; make a thorough list!

What are a few things you could start doing today to live more fully in the fear and wisdom of the Lord?

God's promises to us when we grow in godly wisdom are extensive: prolonged life, peace, kindness, truth, good reputation, favor before God and man, guidance in the decisions we make, avoidance of evil, health, strong bones and body, plenty to eat and drink, prosperity in agriculture (career), long life, riches, honor, happiness, discretion, strength in your life's direction, fearless, looking forward to the future, optimistic, sweet sleep, protection, generous, sharing, helpful, kindhearted, helpful to neighbors, not contentious, intimacy with God, grace, inheriting honor, blessed by God.

In many ways the list of benefits of growing in godly wisdom and the list of characteristics of the Proverbs 31 Woman are similar. The Proverbs 31 Woman is excellent precisely *because* she fears the Lord and has grown in His wisdom and understanding. Her excellence does not come from her own merits and abilities. Her identity is in the Lord, because her source of strength comes from her fear of the Lord.

As you respond in worship to what God is showing you, please listen to "Everything" by Tim Hughes on the "Holding Nothing Back" album. As you envision Christ living in you as your hope of glory, allow Him to gently reveal to you things in your life you value more than Him. Will you lay that thing down, placing Him first? Ask Him to be your Everything!

2

Hannah – My Identity is in My Work
1 Samuel 1:1-28
1 Samuel 2:1-11

We have all used the expression, "So-and-so is very successful." Perhaps this has been said of you or you wish it would be said of you! What do we mean when we say that someone is "successful"? Typically we mean that someone has a job that allows him or her to make enough money to live very comfortably and without financial worries. Not really knowing anything about how satisfying the work is, or whether this person feels particularly gifted to do this work, many of us are quick to define that person as successful.

From the beginning of time, even before the Fall, man was created to do good work. God placed man in the Garden of Eden, which was their place of fellowship with one another, with the very purpose of cultivating and keeping the garden. (Genesis 2:15) Their work was not a curse, but rather a joy, as it was akin to the duties of a priest: tending to the physical place where mankind worshipped God. Paul reminds us in Ephesians 2:10 that part of our purpose in life is to do the work that *God* has intended for us to do. Often, however, we don't take the time to ask Him what work He has intended for us and we end up doing whatever seems right to *us*. When we are living without a greater purpose, we can feel adrift, anchorless in a vast sea of futility. Our work is meant to be an offering to God, as Paul reminds us in Colossians 3:23, "Whatever you do, do your work heartily, as for the Lord rather than for men."

Ultimately our purpose in life should be to glorify God and to make Him known to others. But somehow we tend to mess things up when it comes to our view of work. In the last several generations work has become something that *defines* us rather than serving as a means to *glorify* God. Women today are all the more challenged because we struggle not just with keeping our work from defining our identity, but also in wrestling with the question of whether or not to work professionally in addition to our work as wives and mothers. Look around you. Many working mothers second-guess their decision to pursue their career and wish they could be home more with their children. Many stay-at-home mothers mourn the loss of their career and wonder if professional opportunities will ever come their way again. Nearly every woman tries to dabble in both—often for financial reasons, but sometimes simply to be able to say, "I work…therefore I have significance".

Somewhere we have gone terribly off-track in elevating work to be more than it was intended to be. All of our work, whether it is lovingly caring for our family, fulfilling our responsibilities in our professional realm, serving in our church, or giving to our community is meant to bring glory and honor to God, not a sense of identity to ourselves.

An early figure in the Bible, Hannah, struggled with this very issue, until she allowed God to define her vision of her work and purpose by how she could bring glory to God instead of bringing glory to herself. Hannah had one big problem in an age where a woman's primary work was bearing and raising children. She was barren.

Read Verse 1 – Why does the writer list all the detail about Elkanah's genealogy? What do we learn about God by seeing these long lists of names?

The God who formed us while we were still in our mother's womb (Psalm 139:13-16) and knows the number of hairs on our head (Luke 12:7) is intimately interested in all the details of our life. One of the details that we notice is that Elkanah is a descendent of Ephraim, the younger son of Joseph. Joseph's own mother, Rachel, the favored wife of his father Jacob, was also barren for many years until God chose to show His power and open her womb. Could there be hope for Hannah in this verse?

Seeing detailed genealogies like this one also remind me that God has a deep *personal* interest in us because He has a plan for each one of us. The prophet Jeremiah tells us that God made you unique, set aside for a specific purpose. "For I know the plans that I have for you," declares the Lord, "plans for welfare and not for calamity, to give you a future and a hope." (Jeremiah 29:11) These specific plans include, but are not limited to, our work.

A long account of God's faithful protection over Elkanah's ancestors reminds me that the God of my past is with me in my present and will be with me still in my future. I love when God reminds us of this truth. Several years ago, just 6 weeks after the birth of my third child, I had to have surgery to remove my thyroid. A few years before, my doctor discovered that my thyroid was enlarged and that two nodules were growing on this already over-sized gland. After watching it closely for 2 years, suspicious that the growths might be cancerous, my doctor decided to operate and remove my thyroid.

The day of the surgery arrived, and off I went to the pre-op room. A few minutes after settling into the bed a young nurse came over to me. She began, "You probably don't remember me but..." I interrupted her with a smile of acknowledgement and a simple, "Yes, I do." She was the student nurse who had assisted at the birth of my second child. She proceeded to tell me that the delivery of my son was the first birth at which she assisted, and it helped confirm her desire to be a labor and delivery nurse. I laughed at the memory, because that was the delivery where the epidural didn't work and in my pain, I actually reached my leg out and kicked my obstetrician! What an impression I must have made on this young nurse! We exchanged a few more words, she wished me well, and off she went to care for one of her patients. In that moment God spoke very clearly and very sweetly into my spirit, "Child, I have provided for you in your past, I am with you now in your present, surely I will be with you in your future. Fear not." He is so very generous to remind us of His eternal and transcendent love for us.

Please read vs 2 and briefly describe the two problems in Hannah's life.

Genesis 2:24 says that a man was to have one wife, but Israel did like the other nations around them and took multiple wives. It doesn't take a genius to understand why God would instruct His people to have only one wife. Women are not exactly known for functioning well in 3-way relationships!

In Genesis 1:28 God instructs mankind to be fruitful and multiply. In Psalm 127:3-5 Solomon gives us this insight into how God views children: "Behold children are a gift of the LORD; the fruit of the womb is a reward. Like arrows in the hand of a warrior, so are the children of one's youth. How blessed is the man whose quiver is full of them." And in Proverbs 17:6 we learn that grandchildren are a crown to old men.

At the time during which these verses were written, all societies were agrarian societies, meaning most people worked the land in order to survive. Multiple generations lived together under one roof, and entire families worked together to provide for their basic needs. Children and grandchildren were needed to help tend the land and livestock. There was no social security; grown children were needed to care for elderly parents. If children are considered a blessing from God, how was a lack of children viewed? Not to have children was considered a real stigma, viewed as a curse from God. Hannah was not fulfilling her role of providing children to her family with Elkanah.

Elkanah *had* children—through Peninnah. We don't know which wife came first; we can assume it was Hannah because her name is listed first. We can also assume that perhaps Elkanah took a second wife in order to have children. We do know that he loved Hannah (1:5). The text doesn't say this about Peninnah. We know that he treated Hannah preferentially (1:4-5) even though she was barren. Peninnah is undoubtedly younger, and has at least 4 children (1:4 says "all her sons and daughters").

Imagine how Hannah must have felt. Feel her pain. Describe how she must have felt not having the job of raising children given the norms of her society.

How about you? Did you ever struggle through the anguish of infertility?

How often do we feel like Hannah in our highly competitive world? Do you ever feel regarding your work that you have "missed your calling" and it's too late now to do anything else?

In a world where women now seem to "do it all", do you ever feel like you're not measuring up? Do you ever yearn for work that feels or *appears* more worthwhile than "just mothering"? (Notice how mothering has gone from being *the* career to being viewed as almost no career at all!) Describe some of these feelings.

In verse 3 we are told that Elkanah and his entire family go up to Shiloh every year to make their sacrifices to God. Shiloh, located in Ephraim, is the place of the Tabernacle, the tented, moveable House of God, the place where heaven and earth intersected and God would meet with His people through the high priest.

From the very beginning of creation, God has desired to be in relationship with us; it is in fact the reason for His creating us. We observe this in the first account of humankind as recorded in the book of Genesis. In the Garden of Eden, God walked among His children and enjoyed sweet fellowship with them. And yet, even in that idealized setting, the first humans chose willfulness over obedience and rejected God's order for them. In our human nature, we continue that pattern of selfish living, disobeying and severing our relationship with our holy God. But God is a relentless lover who continues to pursue us despite our faithlessness.

In Eden, God literally dwelled among His people. He walked with Adam and Eve in the cool of the day. It has always been His desire to dwell among us and not be separated by the veil distinguishing heaven from earth. One of my favorite names for Christ is Emmanuel, meaning "God with us". God desires so deeply to be *with* us, that He not only sent His Son to live among us and die for us, but He sent His Spirit to actually take up residence within us, to empower us and fill us with the mighty presence of God so that we can enjoy a permanent state of God's dwelling among and within us.

Between Eden and the first advent of Christ, God makes repeated advances to His people in order to dwell among them. After the Exodus from Egypt, when the Israelites were wandering in the desert for 40 years, God instructs Moses to build the Tabernacle, where He could *tabernacle or dwell* among His people. (Exodus 25:8) He is to be their king and there He will speak through His prophets (like Moses) and His priests (like Aaron). In the wilderness and after they were settled in the Promised Land, the Tabernacle was His dwelling place. Eventually this tented tabernacle will be replaced by a permanent Temple which Solomon, the third king of Israel will construct in Jerusalem. But at the time of Hannah's great anguish, the Israelites' House of Worship—the place of the Presence—is still the tented tabernacle and it was physically located in the town of Shiloh. The tabernacle will figure greatly in Hannah's story, not only because it is there that she will cry out to God from the depth of her pain, but also because her son Samuel will grow up to be an early prophet and priest of the Lord at Shiloh.

Read verses 3-7. Why do you think year after year Peninnah would taunt Hannah as they went to the Tabernacle? Isn't this supposed to be a place of worship? Why does Hannah's infertility keep coming up on these trips?

I imagine that some of their prayers and sacrifices would have been regarding their children: thanksgiving for them, forgiveness for their sins, and protection over them. Year after year, Hannah had to suffer through this very visible reminder that she had produced no children for her husband. If Peninnah, who is referred to in verse 6 as Hannah's "rival", felt less loved than Hannah, she probably would have taunted Hannah in order to prove her own worth over Hannah's. Imagine the dysfunction in this family unit for a minute. Hannah is loved more; yet Peninnah is the one who gave Elkanah children. They were indeed complete and total rivals!

Peninnah is jealous of Hannah being loved more, so she verbally attacks her. Describe a time when you were in Hannah's shoes and someone persisted in verbally attacking you out of jealousy.

Describe a time when you acted like Peninnah, and out of jealousy or insecurity found yourself in a pattern of criticizing someone more vulnerable than yourself.

How about in your professional life—have you been jealous of someone else's promotion or recognition? How did you respond?

When I read verse 8, I'm not sure whether to laugh or cry at Elkanah's naivete! God calls us to be one with our husbands but He has also formed us to desire to be productive and fulfilled apart from them. (Think back to our Proverbs 31 Woman.) Hannah loves her husband but she wants a role, a purpose of her own. She longs for a meaningful career. She craves fulfillment.

Read verses 9-11, 15-16 and describe everything you notice about Hannah's prayer.

It appears Hannah did something unusual in going to the tabernacle. The family had most likely already been to the tabernacle together, returned to where they were staying, eaten a meal together, and then Hannah arose and returned to the tabernacle alone. When we are really hurting, we have to get alone with God and pour *everything* out to Him. She has recognized her deep need and is not too proud to cry out to Him for help—even if she looks foolish in doing so. He is the giver of all good gifts, but before we can *receive*, we need to *ask*.

Undoubtedly Hannah *has asked* God for a child, many times before. Was this time any different? Pay close attention to what she offers to do with this child she is begging the Lord to give her. Hannah is essentially promising God that if He gives her a son, he will be raised as a Nazarite (not a Nazarene like Jesus, meaning from the City of Nazareth!). In Numbers 6:2-8 and Judges 13: 3-5 we get a better understanding of the Nazarite Vow. In her great faith, Hannah is promising God that her son will be set apart for God's work all the days of his life, and as witness to that, no razor will ever touch his head, nor will wine or any unclean thing ever pass his lips. But part of her promise to God includes giving this longed-for son back to God to serve Him in the Tabernacle *forever*.

How could she offer to give up the one thing she had prayed for? How would she feel like she had a role or a job if she gives up the son for whom she prays? Please reflect on how she would have the strength to do this.

Perhaps she would feel like the stigma or "curse" has been removed. In verses 5 & 6 we are told "the Lord had closed her womb". She must have wondered why. She must have wondered what she had done "wrong". Even when we are living faith-filled lives, it is easy to come to God with an "if...then..." mentality. "If I do right, God will bless me. If I do wrong, He won't bless me." While it is important to daily examine ourselves to understand our sin and confess it, it is dangerous to interpret getting what we want as a sign of God's approval of us and not getting what we want as a sign of God's disapproval of us. That kind of thinking really returns us to the bondage of legalism from which Jesus died to set us free.

God had closed Hannah's womb not because He was displeased with her, but in order to show His power through her. Not just His power in opening her womb, but perhaps more importantly, His power in transforming her heart. She no longer cries out, "give me a child so I can be vindicated!" Her prayer becomes, "give me a child who will bring honor and glory to you oh Lord, and he will serve you, not me, all the days of his life." (In a modern adaptation, the prayer which reads: "Bless my career so I will be respected by others and myself!" might become: "Here's my career, Lord, do with it as You see fit.") In this time of intense communion with God, Hannah has found her identity has shifted from being a mother to being someone who brings glory to God. She is willing to trust God with the child (her career) and refuses to hold onto him too tightly. Because her identity is no longer completely formed by whether or not she is a mother, she is willing to give up the child.

In verses 17-18 how does Hannah respond after she has poured her soul out before the Lord?

_____

As often happens after an intense time of prayer, confession, petition, and filling with the Spirit of God, Hannah's entire disposition has changed. She is able to eat. Her face is no longer sad. She has met with the living God and He has transformed her sorrow into joy and confidence. Perhaps you have witnessed this as well. Someone is hurting from deep physical or emotional anguish and asks for prayer. After a few moving moments of intercessory prayer, the one prayed for has literally been filled with a joy and lightness that can only come from the Lord. This was Hannah's experience.

How about you? Have you ever experienced a time like this in prayer where God transformed your sorrow into a deep sense of joy and confidence in Him? Please describe.

_____

Paul tells us in his letter to the church at Philippi to "Be anxious for nothing, but in everything by prayer and supplication with thanksgiving let your requests be made known to God. And the peace of God, which surpasses all comprehension, shall guard your hearts and your minds in Christ Jesus." (Philippians 4:6-7) When we give Him all of our sorrows and anxieties, He promises to fill us with His peace. Notice the verse doesn't say that we will be at peace when *He answers* our prayers; we will be at peace when *we relinquish the rights* to these worries. Hannah experienced this peace when she relinquished the rights to a child God would give her.

Hannah's deep faith in God being at work in her gives her the strength to keep her promise. Sometimes we ask the Lord for direction (in vocational or other choices), we know He has answered, but then a short time later we waver and ask again for more guidance. In these instances, we need to be like Hannah and act in the strength of what He has already shown us. Even Elkanah knows how difficult it will be for her to give up Samuel that he says in verse 23 that he will pray for her that she will be able to keep her promise. When God has clearly spoken to us about our vocation, we must pray for the strength to act on what He has already shown us, even if it is a scary or difficult path.

Hannah longed for a child. Hannah longed for the work of motherhood. Many of us today long for our work to satisfy us in the deepest places. This shouldn't come as any surprise really, given the performance-driven culture in which we live. We struggled with measuring up as a child, wondering, "are my grades good enough?" "Will I get into a good college and have a successful career someday?" "My friends all seem to know what they want to be when they grow up; what should I do with my life?" The questions go on and on as our culture tells us we need to work ever harder to measure up. If we're not careful, and don't nip these anxieties in the bud, recognizing the fear behind the voices as the work of the enemy, we will continue these patterns into adulthood. In adulthood they will take the form of unrelenting performance anxiety in our careers.

The enemy of your soul has one goal in mind—to prevent you from knowing, in the depth of your being, the unsearchable, never-ending, deep love of the Father for you. And one of his classic ways of doing this is to coax you into believing you aren't worthy of receiving God's love. You're unworthy because you don't measure up, and you don't measure up because you haven't worked hard enough.

As schoolchildren, most of us experienced this scenario: we get one bad grade on a test and we begin the mental assault on our character. "I'm so stupid. I don't know anything. I'll never get into a good college. How will I get a good job?" And so the performance-driven approach to life takes hold. "If I work just a little harder, I will be successful. If I'm successful, I will be worthy. If I'm worthy, then I will be loved."

One of the best gifts we can give our children is to cut off this type of thinking and arm them instead with the knowledge that the real struggle is a spiritual battle—not an academic one. Poor performance is not a determinant of our worth. We need to teach our young ones when they are still in school to cast off the performance pressure around them and embrace the love of God for them. It's the surest way of preventing performance anxiety in their careers when they are adults. But, in order to teach our children, we must first lay aside our own fear of our children not "being successful enough" and we must model to them how we trust God with our own careers.

In your own home, are you modeling performance anxiety or trust in God when it comes to your career? How do you do this?

Are you passing on fears of performance anxiety to your children and if so, what could you do differently?

Hannah does keep her promise and presents Samuel at the tabernacle with the appropriate offerings of thanksgiving as indicated in Numbers 15:1-10. This part of the story always terrified me as a child. The thought of my mother leaving me to live and work in the tabernacle with a total stranger really unnerved me! I wonder how Samuel must have felt. I wonder how Hannah felt, since we learn that Eli didn't do such a great job raising his own sons.

Read verses 12-14. What does Eli think is Hannah's problem?

_____

It is interesting that Eli jumps so quickly to this conclusion. Read 1 Samuel 1:3 and 2:12-17 to learn more about Eli's sons. His sons were "scoundrels", probably taken to drunken behavior. Eli was so accustomed to seeing this sort of behavior that he jumped to the conclusion that Hannah was drunk when she was crying out to God. Imagine how difficult it was for Hannah to leave Samuel there with Eli as his one main parental figure.

If you work in a secular environment, is it difficult to imagine that God can be glorified in your workplace through you?

_____

God was with Samuel from even before his birth, and through him, God began to speak to His people again. Samuel grows up to be a priest of the Lord, and the first message he will have to deliver to Eli is that God is so displeased with Eli's sons that they will be destroyed. (1 Samuel 3: 12-14) In addition to being a great messenger of the Lord, Samuel was used of God to anoint the first two kings of Israel. God was able to do all this and more through Samuel because Hannah was willing to give up her rights to her son (her work) and place her "career" in God's hands.

As we think about how Hannah could leave her precious, long-awaited son Samuel at the tabernacle, read chapter 2: 1-10 and describe how Hannah views God.

How does knowing God like this allow us to place our hope and identity in Him?

Read 1 Samuel 2:18-21 for the "end of the story". God richly blesses Hannah, more than she could have ever possibly imagined. But first, she had to be willing to offer everything she had to the Lord, even how she defined herself in terms of her work. Hannah declares in 1 Samuel 1: 27-28: "For this boy I prayed, and the LORD has given me my petition which I asked of Him. So I have also dedicated him to the LORD; as long as he lives he is dedicated to the LORD." Hannah *chooses* to bring glory to God rather than to herself. Our work, whether paid or unpaid, in the home or out of the home, in the church or in the community, highly fulfilling or rather menial is all to be dedicated to the Lord. It is only when we view our work as an opportunity to glorify God that we will be freed from the temptation to let our work define our identity.

As you respond in worship to what God is showing you, please listen to "Love is Here" by Tenth Avenue North on the "Over and Underneath" album. Will you give God your work as an offering for Him to use? Will you trust in His love to satisfy you in the deepest places? Receive His great love for you and rest in that today.

3

Rebekah – My Identity is in My Child's Success

Genesis 24: 10-19, 54-67
Genesis 25: 19-34
Genesis 27: 1-46

We've all met our fair share of Rebekahs—those women who push and prod and promote to ensure that their child gets ahead. Travel team sports champion, honor roll scholar, musical genius, or university athletic scholarship recipient—we all know the prizes and we all know who is winning them and who is not. As parents today we are obsessed with proving our own self-worth by bragging about the accomplishments of our children. Somewhere along the way we have ceased allowing them to live their lives while we live our own; our very identity has become wrapped up in their success as they fill the deepest longings of our souls. The Bible has a word for things that take the place of God in our lives and it is this: idolatry. That's not a word we hear very often in modern society, nor do we expect to hear it associated with our sweet children. But when our children's successes take top priority in our lives, they have most likely become an idol to us. The Free Dictionary defines an idol as "a false god; one that is adored, often blindly or excessively." Sound like any parents you know today, perhaps even yourself at times? How will we ever find our identity grounded in Christ if we are so busy striving for the success of our children?

One of the early figures in the Bible, Rebekah, was so consumed with the advancement of one of her children that she was even willing to sacrifice the good of another one of her children in order to accomplish her goals. We meet Rebekah in the accounts of the Patriarchs of Israel in the book of Genesis. Abraham, the first Patriarch, is called by God to be the father of a new nation, a nation God intends to be a light, or a nation of priests, to the whole world. Abraham marries Sarah, who as it turns out, is barren, unable to have children. Barrenness is a recurring theme in the Old Testament. We saw it in Hannah, we see it in Sarah, in Rebekah—Sarah's daughter-in-law, and in Rebekah's daughter-in-law Rachel. As God touches these barren women and miraculously opens their wombs, He displays His creative power over and over again. He loves to bring newness of life where there once was death! Where there is a lifeless womb, He brings a child. He even does this for Mary, when He opens her virginal womb, which could not in itself have produced a baby. Remember Lazarus? (John 11: 1-45) Remember the son of the widow from Nain? (Luke 7: 11-16) Remember Jesus? All restored to life from a state of death. And when we are not fully alive in Christ because our identity is resting in our children's success, God wants to break that bondage and take us to fullness of life as well.

In the first chapters of His narrative to us, God is preparing to reveal His creative power by bringing life into a dead place. Becoming impatient with God's promise of descendants, Abraham and Sarah decide to take matters into their own hands and Sarah sends her maid Hagar to Abraham to bear a child in her name. Hagar gives birth to Ishmael, who becomes the father of the Arab nations. But this was not the child God had promised, and so He waits another 10 years to display His miraculous creative power to Sarah and Abraham. Finally at ages 90 and 100, God opens Sarah's womb and Sarah gives birth to Isaac who will become the father of the Israelite nation. When it comes time for Isaac to marry, Abraham insists a wife be found for him from among their people in Mesopotamia, not from the Canaanites (Genesis 24). Abraham sends his servant back to his homeland,

and after a successful trip, the servant returns with Isaac's cousin Rebekah to be Isaac's wife.

What do we learn about Rebekah from Genesis 24: 10-19, 54-67?

_____

Lovely, kind-hearted, generous Rebekah. Beloved by her husband Isaac. Adventuresome and willing to travel to a new land to marry someone she had never met. A comfort to Isaac after his mother's death. Fresh and young, she would be a wonderful mother. But there was just one problem. She was just as barren as her mother-in-law Sarah had been! Piecing together verses 20 and 26 of Genesis 25, we understand that Rebekah remains barren for 20 years. While not as long as Sarah's infertility, 20 years is a long time to wait for a child.

Have you ever had to wait a long time for God to answer a deeply longed-for prayer? How precious did that for which you prayed become after God granted it to you?

_____

God answers Isaac's prayers and finally Rebekah becomes pregnant with twins.

Read Genesis 25: 19-28. As a mother, describe how you would feel at learning the prophecy given in verse 23.

_____

From verse 26, it seems that even at birth the younger son is already trying to supplant the older son. We read in verses 27-28 that the boys grow to be very different. Esau, like his father Isaac, likes hunting, outdoor activities, and eating wild game; he is a real man's man. Jacob, on the other hand, prefers quieter activities and staying at home, like his mother Rebekah. Whether or not they picked their favorites because of natural affinities or because of the prophecy—with Rebekah favoring the "winner" and Isaac preferring the "underdog", they each picked "their man".

Have you ever felt the sting of being less favored by one of your parents? Describe how that made you feel, and perhaps still makes you feel today.

If you have children, how do you think that has influenced your own parenting?

Imagine the conflict that would arise in a household that exhibited this kind of blatant favoritism. Isaac should have known better than to allow such favoritism to continue in his household. Growing up in a home that was riddled with favoritism, he knew what kind of affect it has on a family. When Isaac was a child, Abraham favored him over Ishmael, and at Sarah's request, actually sent Ishmael and his mother away into the wilderness. Rather than cutting off this pattern of favoritism, Isaac enters into it as both he and Rebekah will pick their favorite. Jacob (their younger son) will go on to pick his favorite son, Joseph, and give him that amazing technicolor dreamcoat; and we all know what mess that brought about!

Favoritism is a recurring theme in the life of the Patriarchs and there is obviously a lot God wants to show us about the dangers of favoritism not just within the family unit, but outside of the family as well when we "favor" our own children so highly above anyone else.

Please read Genesis 25: 29-34; 26:1.

Jacob, whose name means "one who supplants another", begins tricking and supplanting Esau as a young man. Esau sells his birthright, or his legal rights inherited by birth, to Jacob for a bowl of stew. Granted, there was a famine in the land, Esau's hunt must have been unsuccessful, and all he could think about was his physical needs. But God's verdict on Esau is that he "despised his birthright" (Genesis 25:34). Esau's birthright was his claim to all that his father possessed, including all of the promises of God to Abraham. His birthright represented his leadership of a nation dedicated to God, so selling his birthright reveals how Esau was rejecting God and His direction on his life. In Genesis 26:34-35, Esau continues to reject God and His ways by marrying Canaanite women, bringing great grief to his parents.

How could Jacob have been so deceitful toward his own brother? Perhaps his mother constantly reminded him about the prophecy that he would one day rule over Esau and so he felt the birthright was his *destiny*. But even if she never shared the prophecy with her son, by blatantly favoring Jacob over his brother, Rebekah gave Jacob a super-inflated view of himself. Mother and son undoubtedly believed that he deserved to have everything he desired…even if he had to deceive to get it.

Here are a few choice examples of deceit, which like favoritism, also ran deep in this family:

- In Genesis 20, in order to save his own life, Abraham tells King Abimelech that Sarah is his sister, not his wife, risking her purity by essentially telling the king he could have her in his harem
- In Genesis 25, Jacob steals Esau's birthright
- In Genesis 26, in order to save his own life, Isaac tells King Abimelech that Rebekah is his sister, not his wife, risking her purity by essentially telling the king he could have her in his harem (like father, like son!)
- In Genesis 27, Jacob lies and steals Esau's blessing

When we have not placed our trust in God and what He wants to do in and through us, we are at risk of developing habits of favoritism and deceit to get our own way. In his description of clothing ourselves with the armor of God, Paul tells us in Ephesians 6 that the entire suit of spiritual armor is held together by the belt of truth. When we are willing to compromise on the truth, it becomes increasingly easy to shift our identity from being grounded in the Lord to being centered on ourselves. And once our focus has shifted to satisfying our own desires, blatant favoritism of any one of our children over everyone else cannot be too far behind.

Please read Genesis 27.

Focus in on verses 5-17. Notice how *prepared* Rebekah is with her plan. She doesn't just passively allow favoritism in her home, she *actively* promotes "her man" over Isaac's! Do you get the feeling that she has been listening to many conversations between Isaac and Esau at this late stage in Isaac's life, making sure she knows exactly when Isaac will bestow the blessing on Esau?

What in the text makes you think Rebekah has been plotting this type of thing for awhile?

How could she so easily have encouraged such a huge lie?

Isaac asks Esau to hunt *and prepare* the meal for him. Not only does Rebekah allow Jacob to take two choice lambs from their private family stock, she then *prepares* the meal *for* him! She protects Jacob at every turn, not letting him do a thing!

In what ways do you step in and over-indulge your children in hopes that they will get ahead, rather than allowing them to try, fail, and learn on their own?

Notice that neither the lie nor the act of stealing his brother's blessing seemed to bother Jacob—only the possibility of getting caught did! Jacob and Rebekah make quite a pair! Not only is Rebekah ready with her devious plot in a matter of seconds, but she is also prepared to assume all the risk of carrying out such a plan. She recognizes that if they get caught, someone will be cursed, and she is willing to take on this punishment. (Genesis 27:13) Most likely she figures that if she is caught she can lie her way out of it, since there is a family pattern of lying when it is more convenient than telling the truth.

Do you ever lie about or embellish your children's accomplishments to make them look better? How so?

If God told her when she was pregnant that the older would serve the younger, why do you think she resorts to deceit to bring this about instead of trusting in God?

We sense Rebekah's desperation at ensuring her child's success. You begin to wonder how much Rebekah's life and faith were really rooted in God. Proverbs 3:5-6 says, "Trust in the Lord with all your heart and *do not lean on your own understanding.* In all your ways acknowledge Him, and He will make your paths straight."

In what ways was Rebekah "leaning on her own understanding" of her child's future?

In what ways do you do the same thing with your own children when they are experiencing difficulties?

It appears as though Rebekah wants her sons to marry godly women. In Genesis 26:34-35 we learn that she is distressed over Esau's marriages to local women. Certainly these women have caused her a great deal of distress, but her motivation for sending Jacob away is not as pure as she leads Isaac to believe. We the readers are privy to the conversation between Rebekah and Jacob in which she declares to her son, "Your brother Esau is plotting vengeance against you. He's going to kill you...Run for your life to Haran, to my brother Laban." (Genesis 27: 42-43, MSG) Rebekah wants to hide Jacob from his brother without admitting her wrongdoing to Isaac, so quick as a wink she twists her words and crafts a different story for her husband: "If Jacob takes a wife from the daughters of Heth, like these, from the daughters of the land, what good will my life be to me?" (Genesis 27: 46) Rebekah is a seasoned veteran at manipulation in order to advance her dear son.

List several ways that Rebekah uses manipulation to advance her child and therefore "get ahead".

How do we do similar things today, perhaps with more bragging than manipulation?

Today we have replaced birthright and blessing with varsity letters, honor roll, and university scholarships. Society is filled with parents who yearn deeply for these things for their children and speak incessantly of their children's successes in order to prove their own worthiness. How about you? To what extent are your thoughts and plans driven by a desire to see your children succeed?

Ask yourself these two questions to see if your children are defining too much of your identity:
1. Does my child's success equal my success?
2. Do I feel no one can protect my children like I can?
If the answer to either of these questions is "yes", then like Rebekah, too much of your own identity is probably wrapped up in your children rather

than being formed by who you are in Christ.

So often today our own unresolved issues over how much time we spend at our career versus how much time we spend with our children lead us to put too much pressure on our children to succeed. Their success becomes our success. A parent's need to share in the accomplishments and accolades of their children is enormous today and completely unlike anything we have seen in prior generations and in other cultures. When we are surrounded by parents who force conversations to revolve around the athletic, academic, or musical prowess of their child, how can we help but question, "Why isn't my child as successful? Am I measuring up as a parent?"

In what ways do I push for the advancement of my children so that I will look successful to my friends and acquaintances?

———————————————————————————

What changes could I make to focus less on the achievements of my children? How can I focus more on building up "who they are" rather than "what they've done"?

———————————————————————————

Rebekah tried frantically to get her favored child ahead. Why did she do that and why do we do the same thing today? When we find our identity in our kids, we will have an unbalanced need for them to be successful. Their success ensures that they will be "safe"—meaning bright, healthy, happy, financially secure, handsome, and living a life that's pain-free and better than ours. We will also have an excessive need for others to know about the accomplishments of our children. At the heart of this mistaken identity is a lack of trust in God Himself to protect and provide for them.

When we fret and worry over the success of our children we are displaying a great lack of trust in God. It is essential that we remember that God loves our children more than we do and that He has a plan for all those who trust in Him, including our dearly loved children. God has loved your children with an everlasting love (Jeremiah 31:3), which is a lot more than we can say about our own love for our children! He declares in Isaiah 43:1-7 that He would sell the whole world for your child! In the following excerpt from The Message version of Isaiah 43, replace the word "you" with your child's name and read it aloud:

> "Don't be afraid, I've redeemed you.
> I've called your name. You're mine.
> When you're in over your head, I'll be there with you.
> When you're in rough waters, you will not go down.
> When you're between a rock and a hard place, it won't be a dead end
> Because I am GOD, your personal God...
> That's how much you mean to me!
> That's how much I love you!
> I'd sell off the whole world to get you back, trade the creation just for you."

It is so important to remember when we are reading these Biblical promises that they extend to our children as well as to us, and that God *your* father is also God *their* father. He loves them with a pure love and never takes His eye off them!

There have been two very specific times in my life when God asked of me, "Do you love me enough to entrust your child to me?" Both times involved my son Austin, and both count among the worst experiences of my life. The first situation involved a 5-year season of testing that included the following:

-my suspected thyroid cancer that resulted in 2-years of scans and treatments, followed by a full thyroidectomy 6 weeks after the birth of my third child

- an accident cutting open the skin under my oldest son's eye requiring emergency stitches to his orbital

-two job changes for my husband requiring two out of state moves, one of which was the month following my thyroid surgery

-5 cases of Lyme disease between my 3 children in 3 years

-a visit from my in-laws during which my mother-in-law discovered she had an extremely rare form of cancer. They lived with us for the school year so she could receive treatments at Sloan Kettering Hospital in New York City. She died while vacationing in Italy, 3 months after leaving our home.

Surprisingly, to me, my faith remained strong throughout this time of testing. Exhausted—for sure; but angry at God—no. And then, one week before moving from Connecticut to Pennsylvania, my son Austin was diagnosed with type 1 diabetes, the same disease that took my brother's life when he was 8 and has afflicted my sister since she was 16. This felt like such a mean blow! It was so personal; it was MY family's disease. The diagnosis happened one week before moving. Did I happen to mention how much I hate moving and that a crisis always seems to happen right before we move? I felt like God had kicked me in the gut. "Leave my child alone", I wanted to scream!

I heard the lie of the Enemy whisper in my ear: "this is the so-called Christian life?" and I bought it hook, line, and sinker. Feeling like God had abandoned me, I shut myself off from His love. It would be two years before I would find my way back to God, with a faith, a testimony, and a love for Him that is deeper and richer than anything I had known before. But a lingering question still haunted me: how would I respond if something terrible happened to one of my children again?

Eleven years later I would have the opportunity to ask that question all over again. During a family vacation in Costa Rica, Austin was suddenly struck with food poisoning, just after giving himself a large dose of insulin for his mid-day lunch. With a rapidly falling blood sugar and increasing bouts of nausea, it suddenly became clear that Austin was going to be in a life-threatening situation if we didn't act quickly. The next 30 minutes were the longest in my life as I waited for my other son and husband to run along the beach to our hotel and back with the emergency shot of glucose. Within a few hours he was hooked up to an IV in our hotel room, vomiting continuously, and suffering from diabetic distress. The next day as fever set in, the doctor determined we needed to go by ambulance, 4 hours down to a private hospital in San Jose for better treatment and to rule out appendicitis or kidney infection.

During the journey in the ambulance as my son was frightened for his life and I was imagining emergency surgery in Costa Rica, I wrestled once again with God. I turned over in my mind how much I loved Austin and how vulnerable he was. I prayed for his recovery. I prayed for protection. And then The Lord very gently reminded me that He loved Austin so much more than I did and that He had created him with specific purposes in mind. He knew the number of hairs on his head and had accounted for every day Austin would live. Tearfully, I was able to turn my prayers for healing into prayers for God's will to be accomplished in and through Austin. Like a sudden breeze that blows away the morning fog, a great sense of peace and calm washed over me as I gave my son over to His Heavenly Father's care. God's promise to us in Philippians 4:6-7 is true: "Be anxious for nothing, but in everything by prayer and supplication with thanksgiving let your requests be made known to God. And the peace of God, which surpasses all comprehension, shall guard your hearts and your minds in Christ Jesus."

What does it really mean to trust God with my kids? It is a question I find myself asking frequently as one thing after another with my children seems to go in the wrong direction and Plan A quickly turns to Plan B. I can hear God saying again, "You need to trust me with your child." Does trusting God mean trusting that everything will work out? Perhaps you have heard the expression, "It will all work out in the end; if it hasn't worked out, you're not at the end yet." I don't know that I really believe that, because things don't always work out. Sometimes plans get derailed. Sometimes things go terribly wrong and your Plan A really does become Plan B or even Plan C. And so what does it really mean to trust God in the midst of all of that turmoil?

When things are falling apart in our children's lives, I believe God is inviting us to go deeper with Him. He beckons us to draw near enough to Him to hear His voice. "Do you trust that I am still at work? Do you trust that I am still creating something here? Do you trust that I am not yet finished with the one whom you hold so dear, whose life is going in the wrong direction? Do you trust that even if your child doesn't yet know me, that I'm still trying to reveal myself to your child? Do you believe that I can bring beauty out of ashes?"

Our God first revealed Himself to us as the Creator. To begin the story of His revelation to us with the story of creation reminds us that He is a creative God. He is always at work; He is always busy creating. He never rests. And His watchful eye is always on your child.

At times He may be calling us to wait on Him, fervent in prayer but not taking any action. At other times, He may be calling us to formulate a plan and take action—not like a crazed, worried control freak—but as one who is trusting in God's hand to guide.

To be embraced by the Father and resting in His love is the "safest" place for our kids to be. Things won't always work out the way we had hoped for them, and we might never understand why things have turned out as they did. But the question is, "can we entrust them to the Father's care?"

How can I practice entrusting my children to God's care and viewing their successes and failures as part of God's plan for their lives?

Instead of spending so much mental energy and time focused on advancing our children for their own earthly gain, we should develop the habit of praying and encouraging them to love The Lord their God with all their heart, soul, mind, and strength. (Luke 10:27) In His Sermon on the Mount, Jesus himself instructs us that when we seek His kingdom as first priority in our lives (or our children's lives) a whole host of other blessings will be ours as well. Everything—from our daily needs, to our occupation, to our appearance, to our clothing, to our sense of freedom and meaning in life—God will provide for us. (Matthew 6:25-33) This is great news and is enormously refreshing in a world gone mad over striving for our children's earthly successes!

What changes could I make to my actions and attitudes toward my children to focus more on their spiritual growth and less on their earthly gain?

Rebekah never gets the opportunity to ask herself that question. Thinking he would return in a matter of a few days (Genesis 27:44), Rebekah sends Jacob away to protect him from Esau's anger. Rebekah pays heavily for her deception as Jacob stays in Haran for 20 years (Genesis 31:38), seeking a wife for himself and being deceived along the way. Rebekah's misplaced sense of identity costs her dearly as she will die without ever seeing her precious son again. (Genesis 35:27-29)

As you respond in worship to what God is showing you, please listen to "Lead Me to the Cross" by Hillsong United on the "All of the Above" album. Remember how much Jesus loves you. Can you count everything you hold dear, even your children, as loss, when you reflect on His incomparable love for you? Ask Him to rid you of yourself as you lay everything down and come to the cross, remembering His gift of love poured out for you.

Leah – My Identity is in My Beauty

Genesis 27: 42-44; 28: 1-5
Genesis 29: 1-35
Genesis 30: 1-25
Genesis 32: 3-8; 33: 1-2

Beauty…that ephemeral quality after which women desperately seek, which is said to have ignited the Trojan War, and which lines the pockets of the leading cosmetics companies and plastic surgeons. It is said to be in the eye of the beholder, and yet there seems to be at least a minimum standard by which all people judge it. Does anyone really believe Confucius when he declared: "Everything has beauty, but not everyone sees it"?[3]

Women, especially, strive to be called "beautiful". Why is a focus on beauty so dangerous anyway? Like money, beauty seems to be one of those things that we just can't seem to get enough of! Seriously, have you ever met anyone who thought they were either too rich or too beautiful? When we pursue beauty, we will never be fully satisfied and we will always be left wanting more. Striving for beauty inevitably leads to games of comparison, which lead us to judge others based on appearances. Tolstoy astutely comments in *The Kreutzer Sonata*: "It is amazing how complete is the delusion that beauty is goodness."[4] God tells us instead of pursuing beauty that our adornment should be "the hidden person of the heart with the imperishable beauty of a gentle and quiet spirit, which in

God's sight is very precious." (1 Peter 3: 4, ESV) We will never find our identity fully rooted in Christ if we are constantly seeking after external beauty.

Leah is one of the main figures in the early story of the Patriarchs—those figures in the Old Testament who introduce us to God's enduring love for his beloved children. Like many of us, Leah has to learn the hard way how to find her identity in God rather than in her physical appearance. Leah is the granddaughter-in-law of the first of the patriarchs, Abraham. As we saw in the last chapter, Abraham and Sarah's son Isaac marries Rebekah and they have twin boys Esau (the elder) and Jacob (the younger). God makes it clear that His covenant promises will continue through the younger son, going contrary to ancient law and custom. Jacob will marry two of his cousins: Leah, in a forced marriage, and her younger sister Rachel, because he loves her.

There is a lot of reading in the rich account of Leah and her search for her identity. God graciously gave us this in-depth look into her spirit so that we might benefit from the lessons she learned. We will break the reading down section by section and talk about each as we go along.

Please read Genesis 27: 43-44 and 28:1-5.

For what two reasons does Jacob flee Canaan and go to his mother's homeland?

1.

2.

Isaac, and in particular Rebekah, were very concerned about their sons marrying the local godless Canaanite women. (See Genesis 27: 46.) Their older son Esau had already married a Canaanite woman, which greatly distressed his parents (see Genesis 26: 34-35). They send Jacob to

Rebekah's family to protect him from Esau's anger over stealing his rightful blessing of inheritance and to prevent Jacob from marrying a local godless woman. Keep in mind though, Rebekah's family is not necessarily following the One True God. God has revealed Himself to Abraham and Isaac at this point. Rebekah had been taken OUT of her family and introduced INTO the God of Abraham and Isaac. There is nothing to indicate in scripture that Rebekah's family is God-fearing. In fact, we do know that her family worshipped idols and that perhaps Rebekah still believed in their power. (See Genesis 31:19.) But certainly to Isaac and Rebekah, the women from her family appeared to be better marriage options than the local women.

Please read Genesis 29: 1-31.

Reread verses 16-17. We are not sure what "weak eyes" means. Perhaps her eyes were too close-set and distorted the balance in her facial features. Perhaps she had vision difficulties. Perhaps she squinted and screwed up her face in an age before corrective eyewear made clear vision possible. Whatever the case, clearly Leah was not as beautiful as Rachel.

Describe how it would feel to be Leah.

_____

Reading verse 18, do you assume that every new suitor would prefer Rachel over Leah? What are some feelings you may have toward your sister if you were Leah?

_____

Have you ever felt like Leah either because of a sister or a friend whom you felt was more beautiful or had a better body type than you? Please take a moment to remember and describe what this was like for you.

When I was a young child and teen I was definitely lacking in form and face! I was the girl called "four eyes" in an age when the over-sized frames of the 1970s looked especially ridiculous on my tiny, skinny face. I wouldn't reach 5' tall until I was in high school and I didn't even pass 100 pounds until I was 16 years old. Because my mother preferred the curly hair of my two older sisters to my poker straight hair, I would sleep in rollers every night...until she suggested I get a permanent wave that is! The permanent wave was a disaster—it turned my faux curls into frizz—so I still had to use those crazy pink rollers every night just to calm down my wild hair! Can you just picture the whole image with me? Years of this definitely gave me a sense of being, well...little. Insignificant. The baby. Unimportant. Ugly. And one who simply did not measure up to the beauty and poise of my older sisters and my friends. And yet, all the while, I had a sense of being loved and cherished by my heavenly Father.

In the summer between 10th and 11th grades, my transformation into womanhood would begin. In 4 months I grew 6 inches, got contact lenses, and grew out my hair and let it go naturally straight and long. But it would be years, decades even, before I was able to shake off the identity of the small, insignificant, unlovely little girl that I saw myself as when I was a child and teenager. Our struggles with our identity are often so very deep-seated that they can take years of prayer and Bible study to overcome.

Back to the story at hand...Jacob has no bride price to offer, so he offers to work for his mother's brother, Laban, for 7 years in order to marry Rachel. Jacob was so in love with Rachel that the seven years "seemed but a few days." (29: 20)

How does Laban trick Jacob? Does Laban's trickery remind you of anything or anyone we have already examined?

If you were angry at Jacob for tricking his brother Esau out of his birthright and his blessing, you might be shouting, "What goes around comes around!" You'll find a lot of lies, deceit, and tricks in this family, from Abraham, to Isaac, to Jacob and his children. Are you surprised that God didn't pick cleaned-up individuals to spotlight in His scripture? That's what makes them so fascinating to study—they are sinful and full of warts and all. Because they are just like us, we can learn a lot from them.

Imagine being Leah. Seven years have passed since Jacob first arrived in Paddan-Aram. Seven years on and she is still not married and Rachel is still the favored, the beautiful, the cherished one. Leah is not getting any younger. Any local prospects for marriage have surely been examined and cast aside. Don't you wonder at what point in the 7 years that Jacob served him Laban devised this plan to switch his daughters on the wedding night? Was it his fallback plan all along if a suitor for Leah couldn't be found, or a last-minute act of desperation? At what point was Leah made aware of the plan? Well in advance or that very morning? While it was clearly her father's idea to arrange the deceitful last minute switch of brides, Leah must have on some level hoped that the plan would succeed. She does not want to be caught; but this might be her only remaining chance at marriage.

Imagine the wedding night with me. Leah is veiled. There is nothing but candlelight. Imagine her fear. Imagine her explaining why she wants to leave her veil on, or why she wants all the candles snuffed out. Does she feign modesty? Does she ply him with more wine to dull his senses? Once the act is done and the marriage is consummated, there will be no turning back. She will be a married woman. Jacob will be her husband.

Laban's trick is discovered and Leah's real trials begin. What exchange does Laban make with Jacob? Describe Leah's new position in her new family with Jacob.

_____

Leah is in a very difficult position. While she has finally thrown off her cloak of shame from still being single, she can't really rejoice in the love of her husband. In verse 30 we see that Jacob still very clearly loves and adores her sister and not her. Verse 31 goes on to say that Leah is "unloved", or as some translations put it, "hated". There is no honeymoon period for a hated bride. Leah must have wondered whether she should have refused to go along with her father's plan, for surely her life was now on a course to misery. She had no one to comfort her, not even the Lord, because most likely Leah hadn't yet personally met the Lord God. Yahweh has appeared to Abraham, Isaac, and Jacob—but this is Rebekah's family. They will only know of Yahweh what Jacob reveals to them. She didn't know Him as the God who will "be gracious to whom He will be gracious, and will show compassion on whom He will show compassion." (Ex 33:19) But she was about to meet Him!

What happens next would be humorous if it weren't so sad. Please read Genesis 29:31- 30:24.

Notice that the Lord has compassion on Leah *because* she is unloved, hated even. He opens her womb and allows her to conceive many children, while her sister remains unable to conceive. We can learn a lot about Leah and her relationship with God by looking at the names of her children. By now Jacob must have introduced Leah and her family to the Lord, because her first children are named with references to Yahweh, the One True God.

List the names of Leah's first four sons and write the meaning of the name next to it. What transformation happens in Leah by the time she has her fourth son?

1.

2.

3.

4.

These last few verses have seemed like a race, a wild race for Leah to win Jacob's love and devotion. Leah is by no means unique in hoping that giving her husband a baby will rekindle a spark of love in their failing marriage relationship. Her hope leads to disappointment. Not once, not twice, but three times. And then finally comes baby #4, Judah, whose name means "This time I will praise the LORD." You get a real sense that Leah has finally moved to the place where God has wanted her to be all along: the place of praise. The last line of the chapter reads like a giant sigh of relief: "Then she stopped bearing." Leah has come to realize the secret to keeping jealousy from eating at her to the point of destruction: she praises the LORD.

What jealousies and social competitions are eating at you? How might praise end this cycle of jealousy?

Sometimes there's nothing like the old King James Version to really drive a point home. There, Isaiah 26:3 reads: "Thou wilt keep him in perfect peace whose mind is stayed on Thee." That's a promise if I ever heard one! When we keep our minds focused on Him, he promises to be our peace. When we focus on Him, we take our eyes off ourselves. With our thoughts centered on Him, we can't help but move into times of praise. How do we keep our mind focused on Him and not on our own feelings of insecurity? The second half of Isaiah 26:3 tells us how: "because he trusts in Thee." It begins with trusting God to meet our needs—not necessarily giving us everything we ask for—but meeting our needs. Ultimately what Leah really *needed* was to experience and rest in the unconditional love of her heavenly Father; what she *kept asking for* was love and acceptance from her husband. As we learn to trust God to meet our needs, then we need to practice thinking about God as we go about our day. Yes that's right; think about Him! Dwell on His goodness and mercy. When we find our minds drifting back to our own worries, we must learn to reel them back in, back to the place where our mind is "stayed on Him". When we do this, we will find God's peace, even when our own situation hasn't changed.

Soon it is Rachel's turn to grow increasingly jealous of Leah. Imagine Rachel watching and waiting and frantically calculating which nights she must be with Jacob to become pregnant, even as her sister bears one son after another to the husband they share between them. Chapter 30 is one long, sad competition between the sisters to win their husband's love and in so doing to elevate their own stature within the family and community as a whole. At least 14 years will pass and 13 children will be born as this struggle to be the favored one plays out.

Notice that, like Sarah, both Rachel and Leah offer their handmaids to their husband to bear children in their name. Unlike Hannah, who took her problem of barrenness to the Lord in prayer and submission, trusting Him with the outcome, Sarah, Leah, and Rachel frantically seek to fix their problem on their own terms. Because they have each allowed their condition to define them, they are incapable of trusting in God to work mightily through them. And so they each succumb to the desperate act of offering their maids to sleep with their husband. We see from Jacob's angry response in Genesis 30:2 that he was not in favor of manipulating God's apparent will. Jacob would have heard plenty from his father Isaac about the dangerous ramifications of trying to help God along in the baby-making department! When our identity is as misplaced as it was for these women, we will be prone to act out of our insecurity rather than trust in God as our source of strength.

The list of the names of Leah's sons reads like a diary synopsis of her life and emotions. When you look through the meanings of her children's names and her reasons for giving them their names, it is clear that her relationship with Jacob never improved. She always longed for more: to be loved, to connect with Jacob, to be highly esteemed enough in Jacob's eyes to receive gifts from him. We saw the high point in her relationship with the Lord was when she gave birth to Judah, declaring that now she will praise the Lord. But what happens after the birth of this precious son? Does she continue to praise Him to keep jealousy from controlling her? There appears to be a season in her life when she rises above the jealousy, the loneliness, the constant feeling of not measuring up. Look at the list below. Do you see it? Reread the meanings of her sons' names and what do you notice?

Reuben	God has seen my misery; now my husband will love me.
Simeon	God has heard that I was unloved; and so He gave me this son also.
Levi	Now maybe my husband will connect with me.
Judah	This time I will praise God.
Gad	Fortunate. (son of Zilpah)
Asher	A happy day. (son of Zilpah)

Issachar	Bartered - God remembered me for giving my maid to my husband.
Zebulun	Honor – God has given me a great gift. This time my husband will honor me with gifts.
Dinah	Judgment.

Did you notice that after her time of praising God, she *seems* to be happy, viewing herself as fortunate? Unfortunately this isn't a genuine happiness formed from an identity rooted in God. She has given into the temptation to compete with her sister yet again, and these two sons are the sons of her handmaid, Zilpah. In her insecurity, Leah has given into the race to conceive once again, desperate to prove her worth by the number of sons she can give her husband. Leah didn't take the time or necessary action to practice praising God so the high point in her relationship with Him doesn't last.

We see from Leah's personal "diary" that she has allowed her insecurities and her own quest to identify herself outside of her relationship with God to consume her. When we are struggling with issues of identity such as beauty, loneliness, or being loved, we can go one of two ways. We will either go to the place of self-pity—which can lead to more competition and struggle, or to the place of praise. Leah's descendant, the great King David, who comes from the line of Judah, will declare, "You are enthroned upon the praises of Israel" (Psalms 22:3), reminding us that when we choose to praise Him, He takes up full residence within us on the throne of our hearts. This may be difficult doctrine to grasp in the time before Jesus' resurrection and the giving of the Holy Spirit to indwell God's people; but for us today, the exchange is simple and yet profound: we literally step off the throne of our lives and ask God through His Spirit to take up complete rule and reign in our heart and life. This is not a one-time yielding of our heart's throne, but a daily relinquishing of the seat of power in our life. When we do this, we will be able to dwell in the place of praise. Leah's personal story as revealed in the names of her sons points to this very fact: when we choose to praise the Lord instead of giving into self-pity, He will satisfy us in the deepest places.

When you are struggling with discontentedness over your personal appearance—your weight, your face, your figure—what do you typically do to alleviate the pain?

If God has "blessed you in form or face", how much do you, perhaps subconsciously, rely on that as your source of identity and strength, finding your confidence in your personal appearance rather than in your hope in the Lord?

A curious thing happens after Rachel delivers her first child. Jacob suddenly thinks of "going home." Leah has borne Jacob six sons and one daughter, and has given him two more sons by her handmaid, but Jacob only yearns for home after Rachel gives him a son. Even after Leah has given Jacob nine children, did he only feel like he had a family to be proud of after Rachel bore him a son? Oh Leah, I hope you started singing praises to God just then, otherwise I can feel your sense of identity faltering again.

Relations had been strained for some time between Jacob and his father-in-law Laban, and even with his brothers-in-law, who accused him of taking their father's wealth. By Jacob's own account, Laban had changed his wages "ten times". After living in Paddan-aram for 20 years, and at God's prompting, Jacob returns to Canaan, the land of his father. It seems Jacob still hasn't learned to be totally honest though, for he and his family flee Paddan-aram in secret, without telling Laban. Laban pursues Jacob and his family, eventually catching up with them. It was not a friendly meeting, but rather one where they agreed never to see one another again.

Jacob has been with Leah's family for two decades. All this time she has witnessed his undivided love for her sister and his near hatred for her. Would things be different in Jacob's homeland? Might Jacob's mother take pity on Leah and encourage Jacob to love her more and treat her with dignity? Could Canaan be a place of new beginnings and a fresh love between her and her husband? Before they can be welcomed by Jacob's family, Jacob will need to be forgiven by Esau. If Esau can possibly forgive Jacob, might Jacob finally be able to forgive Laban and Leah for tricking him on his wedding night and see Leah with new eyes?

Please read Genesis 32: 3-8, 33:1-2

Jacob continues his journey and sends a messenger to Esau to let him know of his return to the land. Remember, they haven't seen one another in 20 years and the last time they were together, Jacob was fleeing for his life. Jacob's messenger returns announcing that Esau was coming to meet him, accompanied by 400 men! Jacob's response to this news is immediate and visceral: "he was greatly afraid!" (32:7) He and his whole company are trapped—Laban is blocking him from behind; Esau is blocking him from the front. He is trapped. So he sends an offering of flocks and cattle ahead of him to appease his brother whom he had so greatly offended 20 years before.

And then Jacob does a very hurtful thing...if your name is Leah that is. Jacob takes his entire company and arranges them in perfect order—ascending order of his love and devotion to his family members so that the first in line would be the first to be attacked and killed if Esau doesn't relent. The maids and their children are first in line. Then come Leah and her 7 children. And finally Rachel and her son Joseph. If Leah harbored any hope of a new standing in her new land, surely those hopes were dashed as they marched toward Canaan in obvious order of Jacob's affections. Imagine the shame. Imagine the hurt and disappointment. Imagine the jealousy. Feel the ongoing sibling rivalry. All because you have "weak eyes" while your sister is "beautiful of form and face".

How have you allowed your physical features, either good or bad, to form your identity?

The enemy's goal is to take a truth or a near-truth about you and to distort that truth into a falsehood. So for example he might whisper to you, "See that woman standing next to you? You are not as beautiful as that woman." Or "you are fifty pounds overweight", or "your face and body are not aging well". And while those statements may be true, he will then take one of those statements and distort it to a lie such as, "you are therefore unlovely. You are unlovable. No one will love you because you don't measure up to the accepted standard of beauty." And what the Father wants to tell you is that you are perfectly made in His image and that He has a covenant love with you that is irrespective of anything you do or what you look like. His love for you is steadfast and is freely given.

How do we get to the place where our physical appearance doesn't matter so much to us? As we saw in 1 Peter 3, God's instruction to women is clear: "What matters is not your outer appearance…cultivate inner beauty, the gentle, gracious kind that God delights in."(MSG) How do we get to the place where our internal appearance before God is more important to us than our external appearance before man? We have to start by taking our eyes off ourselves and focusing more on God. When our minds stay fixed on God, and we take every thought captive to the mind of Christ, we will be intentionally stepping off the throne and giving Him access to the throne of our lives. Praising Him, as we saw from the verse in Psalm 22, is another way to ensure that He takes up the seat of honor in our heart.

From a time management perspective, how much more time do you spend on your outer appearance than on your inner beauty, especially your spiritual development?

How much time do you spend looking at and worrying about your changing face and body as you age?

How can a habit of praise help prevent you from fixing your identity on your own outward appearance?

Eventually the sibling rivalry does end, but only at the death of Rachel, somewhere between Bethlehem and Bethel. In an almost ironic end to their rivalry, Rachel dies in childbirth after meeting Esau, but before ever making it to Isaac's home in Hebron. But even though she is Jacob's only remaining wife, Leah still has no hope of establishing a good relationship with her mother-in-law Rebekah. The woman who 20 years beforehand sent her son off to protect him from his brother's vengeance and to find a wife among her family has died long before he returns. Leah will find no advocate in Rebekah.

But all is not lost for Leah. God still remembers her and because He does not play favorites based on "form or face", He chooses to bless her. From Leah comes Judah, and ultimately all the kings of Israel will descend from the tribe of Judah, including David, including Solomon, and most of all, including the greatest Son of David, the Lord Jesus. Jesus, the "Lion of Judah" is the offspring of the son of whom Leah declared, "This time I will praise the LORD!"

By all appearances Leah did not cultivate her relationship with God to the point that her identity stayed rooted in Him. Following the high point after Judah's birth, her identity gradually shifted back to being self-focused rather than God-focused. What a shame she didn't rest in what God had shown her about who she was in Him. She could have lived out her days confident in the assurance that in God's eyes she was "fearfully and wonderfully made" by a God who knew every hair on her head. Only praising God and keeping our minds fixed on Him will keep us safely in that place of knowing that our true identity is in Him.

As you respond in worship to what God is showing you, please listen to "Beautiful Things" by Gungor on the "Beautiful Things" album. Can you offer Him the pain of the things in your life that are not beautiful? Can you trust that His love for you is enough? Will you trust that the God of all creation can make beauty out of dust, beauty out of ashes, beauty out of chaos, beauty in you?

5

Eve—My Identity is in Being Right

Genesis 1: 26-28
Genesis 2: 7-9, 15-25
Genesis 3: 1-24

Let's face it, nobody likes being wrong, do they? To admit we are wrong somehow hurts our pride, doesn't it? And it's not just admitting our big faults that gives us pause. Sometimes it's admitting the small, stupid mistakes that threatens our pride the most. When our pride prevents us from owning our faults and mistakes, we have no other option but to hide and avoid the truth about ourselves. We cannot live in this kind of denial of the truth and have our identity firmly rooted in God. The two are mutually exclusive.

One of the saddest verses in all of scripture occurs right at the outset of our first encounter with mankind. In verse 10 of Genesis 3, Adam declares to the Lord, "I heard the sound of Thee in the garden and I was afraid...so I hid myself." The Lord God, who is described elsewhere as "loving", "good", "righteous", and "tenderhearted", expressly made man in His image *to be in relationship* with Him, not to be afraid of Him, cowering in the bushes. But that is what can happen to us when we sin before a holy God and refuse to ask forgiveness. We hide—either by running away from God's holy gaze, or we blame someone else for our failure, or sometimes both.

Eden, the place of all beginnings, Paradise, Heaven on earth. Eden was all that and more to Adam, except that he was alone, with "no helper suitable for him". In creating Eve, God opens the door for intimacy in human relationships that is to be akin to our intimacy in our relationship with Him. They were not only *to be* together, they were *to cleave* to one another. That is a very strong word that evokes a sense of attachment—physical and emotional, a dependency, an ease of intimacy that is hard to find even in the best marriages today. When we read that "they were naked and not ashamed", you can be sure that it is not only *bodily* nakedness that is implied. They were raw, laid bare before one another, revealing all that was on their hearts and minds, and yet were not ashamed. This degree of intimacy, where nothing is hidden and everything is honestly exposed can only be possible when we are willing to live transparent lives before God and man in the confidence that we will neither be rejected nor condemned by our heavenly Father.

When we are right before God and man, we feel whole. Accepted. Confident. Secure. The trouble is, we spend so little time actually living right with God and one another that we don't really know what it is to be whole. We sin by offending God or man and then rather than confessing our wrongdoing and quickly returning to right relationship, we ignore it, or make light of it, or pass blame elsewhere, all the while preventing any restoration in relationship from happening. And we wonder why we feel so broken in our relationships!

Recount a time when one of your relationships was wounded, either by avoidance or by blaming, because neither you nor the other party sought full restoration after the offense.

By contrast, recount a time when you actively sought restoration by confessing your wrongdoing. How did that benefit the relationship?

A few years ago, a woman who had been living with type 1 diabetes for more than 20 years underwent a rare procedure called an islet cell transplant in which she received a cadaver's insulin producing pancreatic islet cells. The result was that for the first time in more than 20 years, her body was "whole" and was able to make insulin itself. When asked how she was responding to the treatment she related that she had never realized how poorly she felt every day before the transplant, because she hadn't felt so well in such a long time. We are not too different from this woman when we live in our sin, refusing to admit our wrongdoings to God and one another, and never tap into the wholeness that comes from restored relationships. We become accustomed to relationships that lack intimacy because of brokenness. Setting our identity on being right at the expense of being restored has always been a dangerous game to play, but is one that was played right back at the beginning of time by Eve, "the mother of all the living".

Eve, along with her husband Adam, enjoyed long walks in the garden in the cool of the day with their Father God. There is honesty in their relationship, even as she has security in her identity: she is a child of the Creator. And then in the first verse of Chapter 3, the small word "now" breaks through and changes everything. "Now the serpent was more crafty than any beast of the field…" Can't you just feel the wind shift as an icy chill blows through the Garden?

Knowing that our enemy is like a lion seeking whom he may devour (1 Peter 5:8), we can be fairly certain that he didn't just ask Eve one time about eating the forbidden fruit before she gave into temptation. No, the conversations probably stretched on for months, years perhaps, and may have gone something like this:

"Eve, did you notice the lovely fruit on the tree over there?"
"I avoid that tree."
"Why?"
"I can't eat that fruit."
"Yes, but did you notice it?"
"I try not to pay attention to it."
"I wonder what a little taste of that fruit would be like?"
"I can't eat that fruit."
"Oh Eve, the fruit smells so good, even from over here!"
"Hmm, you are right; I hadn't noticed its scent before."
"Why don't you just smell it then…smelling isn't tasting, right?"
"I'm not sure."
"Let's just look at it together then, and catch a whiff from time to time as the breeze blows our way."
"I'm not so sure about this."
"Just enjoy the scent as we sit way over here."
"Well, okay…"
"How about a little taste today? A little taste can't be the same as eating the whole thing, right?"
"I'm not sure anymore."
"Why can't you just taste such a pretty fruit Eve?"
"God said I can't eat it."
"Oh really, God said, 'You can't eat from any tree of the garden'?"
"God said I can't eat from the tree in the middle of the garden, or even touch it or I will die."

And this is still how it is when we sin today. We start out committed to a pattern of right behavior and so we avoid behaviors we know to be ungodly: coarse language, excessive drinking or indulgent eating, adulterous thoughts, telling "white" lies, etc. But, if we are more concerned about "right behavior" than a right heart before God, we are at risk of following the ever-shifting changes to our standard and the voice that urges us to conform. Just recall how standards have changed in your own lifetime or that of your parents. As recently as the 1950's, married couples could not even be portrayed on television as sharing the same bed! That standard has certainly shifted enormously. Societal views toward divorce, pre-marital sex, and homosexuality have changed tremendously in the past 40 years alone. Business practices shift and what was once considered unethical is now called a "gray area"…as long as you don't get caught. When we start giving into a worldly standard instead of living by God's standard, eventually we will be unable to remember exactly what God commanded of us, or why.

It starts with a lie. Satan, referred to as "the father of lies" in John 8:44, is quite skilled at taking a mostly true statement, twisting it ever so slightly, and then whispering that lie deep down into our souls. When Satan whispers a lie about us it is all too easy to buy into it and forget God's promises to us. A short time ago a dear friend of mine experienced this sort of whisper to her soul. As she was preparing to send her youngest child off to college, her beloved dog died suddenly of cancer. Since her husband's job takes him away from home Monday through Thursday, she began to hear the whisper, "you are all alone". You see, my friend, whose father abandoned her family when she was a young child, has heard this whisper before. She knows the voice. The sting of "departure" had returned. As we talked, we naturally moved into a time of prayer, claiming the promises that "I will never leave you nor forsake you", and "I have loved you with an everlasting love". Nothing changed in my friend's life to prevent her from experiencing this season of "aloneness", but her identity was restored to being rooted not in the lies about being alone, but rather in the truth about being deeply loved and cherished by her heavenly Father.

So we see Satan's part in whispering lies to Eve, prodding her on to sin. He confuses her about which fruit she can and can't eat so that eventually she declares that she can neither eat nor *touch* the forbidden fruit. God never said anything about not touching the fruit. Satan's lies bring about confusion that sets Eve up to choose to sin.

What can we learn about how Eve was tempted that applies to us today? In verse 6 of chapter 3 Eve makes three observations about the fruit that give us insight into three of our greatest weaknesses as humans, and especially as women. The fruit was good for food, a delight to the eyes, and desirable to make one wise.

- The fruit was good for food. Food here represents all of our physical and material needs. Every woman desires for her physical needs to be met and as a nurturer, longs to know that the physical needs of her family will be met.
- The fruit was a delight to the eyes. Honestly everyone—who doesn't want to be found "beautiful"? At some level, it is something we all long for and in which we judge ourselves quite harshly. A delight to the eyes represents our deep longings for things we don't have.
- The fruit was desirable to make one wise. Wisdom leads to prestige, power, and an elevated role in one's community and so it encompasses our desire to be respected and taken seriously.

Are we really any different from Eve? Proverbs 27:20 tells us that the eyes of man are never satisfied. Aren't these the things that we most deeply desire when we take our eyes off God and His plans for us? When we root our identity in any of these things rather than in our position before God, we are sure to find ourselves walking headlong into a trap of sin.

Which of these desires do you struggle with the most? Physical and material things, beauty and deep inner longings, or wisdom, power and respect? How does that struggle manifest itself in your life?

Describe a time when your yearning in one of these areas was so strong that you were tempted to "take a bite" and give into the temptation.

Can you describe a time when you had victory over one of these struggles?

And so, Adam and Eve willingly chose to disobey God. This account of the first sin reveals that God does not tempt us. Eve was drawn away by her desire for the fruit and what it would give her. Her desire, which was fueled by Satan, gave birth to sin. James reminds us that God cannot be tempted by evil and so He does not tempt us with evil (James 1: 13-15). The players in the drama are we humans, Satan, and our desires.

When we devote too much of our attention to our unmet needs—whether it's physical things we long for, or deep inner desires, or an unquenchable thirst for wisdom and power—we become acutely aware of our own insufficiency. The more we dwell on our unmet needs—those things we hunger for and earnestly desire—the greater will be the weight of our insufficiency. When we are consumed by the burden of constantly trying to measure up, we can have a tendency to want to prove our worth by being right. When we feel vulnerable, we move into self-protection mode, refusing to be found at fault, always needing to be right.

And so we blame others when things don't go as we planned. Or we become defensive when we feel we are being wrongly accused. All because we feel the weight of our own insufficiency and a great need to prove ourselves. In the secret places of our heart we hear the whisper, "I don't measure up so I must prove to you how smart I really am…how right I am…how good and worthy of love I am."

Eve was ripe (pardon the fruit pun!) for falling into the trap of sin. Please understand, Eve is guilty of having chosen to sin. She was, however, all the more likely to sin because she was not careful to avoid the trap of focusing on her unmet needs. She was hungry—and not just for fruit! She was hungry in the deepest places of her heart. Instead of taking her deepest needs and desires to the Lord, she tried to satisfy them with earthly things, things that will never—can never—satisfy. Eve discovered what we all discover when we disobey God in an attempt to have our deep needs met—that the thing we experienced in our disobedience does not satisfy.

As soon as Eve willfully disobeyed she felt the sting of shame. She and Adam had been naked all along, but suddenly, they were ashamed. Outright disobedience always exposes us and opens us up to shame and fear. So we cover up, or we blame, both of which only lead to more trouble.

Can you identify occasion(s) when you were feeling particularly "insufficient" and you felt a need to prove your worth by showing what you knew?

Can you identify some root causes of defensiveness in your own life? How do you typically play the Blame Game?

_____

Describe a time when your selfish, sinful actions wounded someone else and you entered into the Blame Game. Rather than feeling better about yourself, how did your feelings of self-righteousness lead to isolation in the relationship?

_____

Because the Blame Game fuels our desire for self-protection, it will always result in broken intimacy rather than in restored relationship. When we engage in the Blame Game, we keep our eyes focused on ourselves and not on the other person or on God, blocking the way to confession, forgiveness, and restoration.

At first Adam and Eve work together to literally "cover up". Together they hatch a plan to cover themselves with fig leaves. Imagine the whole production with me. First they have to find these enormous fig leaves. Then they have to find some vines to serve as thread. Then they would sew the fig leaves together, making a means of attaching them to their bodies. Perhaps they even devised a plan for how to respond to God's questions about their new fashion statement! This elaborate scheme must have taken them far longer to carry out than their act of sin did! And then, in the ultimate act of shame in the face of a holy God, they hid. And they waited.

From the beginning of time, this is how we all respond to God when we refuse to confess our sins immediately. David cries out in Psalm 15: "O LORD, who may abide in Thy tent? Who may dwell on Thy holy hill? He who walks with integrity, and works righteousness, and speaks truth in his heart. He does not slander with his tongue, nor does evil to his neighbor, nor takes up a reproach against his friend." When we do not walk in integrity, when we do not speak the truth, when we slander one another, we cannot abide in God's holy presence. And so we hide from Him. And because God is a relentless lover who will always pursue us in order to restore relationship with us, He comes after Adam and Eve and questions why they are hiding.

Have you ever been in a situation where you felt like you wanted to hide from God because of things you had done? Please describe the situation and how you pulled away from Him.

Adam starts out well by answering God in the first person singular, accepting his part in their actions: "I heard the sound of Thee in the garden, and I was afraid because I was naked; so I hid myself." But as soon as God turns up the heat and questions him further, the Blame Game begins. God asks Adam two direct questions. It is the moment of truth, an opportunity to fess up and come clean. "If we confess our sins, He is faithful and just and will forgive us our sins and cleanse us from all unrighteousness." (1 John 1:9) *God convicts us not to condemn us but to correct us.* Our confession always brings about restoration. Ever notice how the demeanor of a child who has just broken something that didn't belong to him changes once he has the opportunity to confess and ask forgiveness? The parent just knows something is wrong by looking at the child—he has a guilty, slinking look about him. He becomes quiet and withdrawn. The parent notices and questions. The child confesses. The parent forgives. The child skips off light-hearted. It is forgiven. It's over.

But we adults don't often do this. Instead we squirm and try to hide, or if that doesn't work, we pass the blame onto someone else. Anyone else, as long as it's not ourselves. Adam does not confess and come clean; he blames not just Eve, but God as well when he says, "the woman *You* gave to be with me, she gave me from the tree and I ate." How audacious to blame God for our own choices! God then turns His direct questioning to Eve asking, "What is this you have done?" And without missing a beat, Eve declares, "the serpent deceived me!" It's a wonder she didn't say, "the serpent *whom You made* deceived me!"

When we don't own our mistakes, shortcomings, and outright sins, we either cover up and hide ("it's not that bad", "everyone's doing it", "I'm not as bad as some people") or we blame others. In either case, it is our pride that prevents us from being honest and causes us to hide or pass blame. We hide from God by withdrawing from His presence. We hide from man by withdrawing from the one we have offended. When we cease being honest with ourselves and choose to be defensive instead, we blame anyone or anything rather than accept the responsibility ourselves. To be that person of integrity that David speaks of, we must be honest and bare before God, and we can't be bare if we're hiding things or blaming others for our actions.

Let's face it, in our society today, it is rare to find people who consistently accept responsibility for their actions. Even our language reflects our unwillingness to be found at fault. Instead of saying, "I'm sorry, you are right, I'm wrong", the common retort is now, "my bad". Or when a school age child forgets his homework, the parent immediately rushes it over to the school office so the child won't have to accept any responsibility for his forgetfulness. And when we adults recognize a habitual sin pattern in ourselves, we are all too likely to pass the blame onto our parents, our upbringing, or our circumstances rather than to accept our own part in cultivating this behavior and ultimately our responsibility for correcting it. Why are we so afraid to admit we are wrong? Are we afraid we'll look bad? Are we afraid there will be no forgiveness?

How difficult is it for you to admit when you are wrong? How hard is it for you to say you are sorry?

Are there some people to whom it is very difficult to admit you are wrong? Why do you think this is?

Is it easier or more difficult to confess your wrongdoing to God? What keeps you from confessing your sin to God?

Very often, wounds from our past lead to the protective behaviors of blaming others, defensiveness, bragging, and sarcasm. At one time or another, we all experience some measure of threat to our sense of self-worth. Perhaps you were bullied as a child or felt insignificant in your family unit. Perhaps you work for a tyrannical boss who takes every opportunity to belittle you. Perhaps you felt over-looked as a child until getting the best grades at school got you noticed, and so you have learned that being "right" gives you power. When we live with unhealed wounds to our self-worth, we will turn-on our self-defense strategies every time we feel threatened. We will do anything we can—blame someone else, make excuses about our behavior, brag about ourselves, speak sarcastically against someone else—to protect ourselves from feeling inadequate.

What unresolved wounds from your past influence the way you cast blame on others today?

Sometimes we're desperate to find someone to blame for something that has gone wrong—we feel like a failure, our child didn't make the team, our child got terribly sick, we didn't get the promotion, etc. We want someone to blame because we need a place to direct our anger, a place to direct our frustration. Sometimes there is no one to blame; it's just life, and life hasn't worked out as we wanted. And so, we make excuses or blame someone else just to have a place to cast our unresolved anger.

Can you recall a time when "life didn't work out as you planned" and you chose the self-defense response of casting blame on others? Please describe.

When you are feeling threatened or insignificant, does criticizing or putting someone else down help you feel better about yourself? Can you recount a specific time when you did this?

Beware—if you are all too quick to make sharp, critical comments about others, or if a fear of being on the receiving end of constructive criticism frequently leads you to respond defensively—you are probably trapped in a long round of the Blame Game. God desires to free you from this trap so that you may find your identity in Him and not in your being "right".

God does forgive Adam and Eve, even though they never ask for His forgiveness. God Himself killed an animal in the first blood sacrifice recorded in the Bible in order to provide skin coverings for Adam and Eve. There is forgiveness, but the sin doesn't come without its consequences. Woman will have pain in childbirth. She will desire deep relationship with her husband but he will rule over her. Man will toil to earn a living. Sin has consequences, and sin requires forgiveness.

It is easy to imagine when God casts them out of the garden that He has rejected them. Why else would He send them away, right? He does not reject them; rather, He casts them out to protect them, to bring about restitution in their relationship with Him. They have sinned in eating of the Tree of the Knowledge of Good and Evil. If they stay in the Garden and eat of the Tree of Life, they will live forever in their sin and never be able to be with God face to face again. You see, they, like we, need to die on this earth in order to be alive again in God's eternal kingdom. God was telling the truth when He told them that they would surely die if they ate of the fruit. Not only did the "dying" process begin in their mortal bodies when they sinned, but death would now be the only way to return to full communion with God after sinning.

How do we maintain a close relationship with God? By "walking with the Lord in the cool of the day", that is, by spending time with Him daily in prayer and in studying His word. How do we return to communion with Him after we have sinned and we feel that barrier between us? By confessing and seeking restitution with Him. Remember, God convicts us of wrongdoing to correct us, not to condemn us, in order that we may receive His love and enjoy close fellowship with Him.

As you respond in worship to what God is showing you, please listen to "Hungry (Falling on My Knees)" by Joy Williams on the WOW Worship album. What are you hungry for? Can you give Him your deepest unmet desires and needs? Can you trust Him with your insufficiency and lay down your need to be right? Fall on your knees before the only One who satisfies.

6

Sapphira – My Identity is in My Community Stature (Translation: I Want to be Popular!)

Acts 4: 32-37
Acts 5: 1-11

Can you imagine a community described by these words:

"They were continually devoting themselves to the apostles' teaching and to fellowship, to the breaking of bread and to prayer. And everyone kept feeling a sense of awe; and many wonders and signs were taking place through the apostles. And all those who had believed were together, and had all things in common; and they began selling their property and possessions, and were sharing them with all, as anyone might have need. And day by day continuing with one mind in the temple and breaking bread from house to house, they were taking their meals together with gladness and sincerity of heart, praising God, and having favor with all the people." (Acts 2: 42-47)

Sounds ideal, doesn't it? Could you imagine living in a community where loving-kindness, sharing, humility, and respect were standard rules of behavior? All too often, society today is characterized by a "me-first" attitude, a sense of "I'll help you if it benefits me in some way", and a general lack of humility, fueled by a desire for others to know and recognize our own strengths and contributions. In the description of the early Church given in the second chapter of Acts, God paints a picture of what society can look like when He is at the center.

When you think about your local community, what are some words—both good and bad—that come to mind? (Throughout this chapter, when I ask you to think about your "community", please think about the various communities to which you find yourself belonging: your neighborhood, your town, your workplace, your church, your schools, your extended family, etc.)

How closely do your communities resemble that of the early Church?

If you are honest, how frequently do you fall prey to the trap of helping others only when it is beneficial to you in some way, including the recognition you receive afterward? Can you identify a specific example of this?

The most striking thing about the early church was their unity and devotion to helping one another. They were "of one heart and soul; and not one of them claimed that anything belonging to him was his own." (4: 32) By spending much time with one another, they built a strong sense of community. They were so devoted to each other that their attitude about property and belongings was that they were held for the common good of the group. There was no formal regulation stating that upon conversion they would sell all of their property and give the proceeds to the leaders of the community. Rather, their commitment to Jesus Christ produced in them a changed attitude about their possessions that caused them to view all they had as belonging to God, and therefore they were happy to share with those in need who shared this same love for Jesus. They didn't give out of a desire for recognition of their magnanimous act; they gave because they were motivated by love and a desire to freely give. Because no one claimed that anything he owned belonged to him alone, there was not a needy person among them. It is extremely important to understand that no one was under any compulsion to sell his property in order to join this community. Decisions to sell one's property in order to help another were private matters between the property holder and God. In our private decisions, God calls us to act out of integrity and honesty. Our all-seeing, all-knowing God can see right through any pretense as He gets straight to the real motivation for our actions. As always with the Lord, it is the hidden condition of the heart that matters.

Those who chose to sell their property for the benefit of the community would "bring the proceeds of the sale and lay them at the apostles' feet." (4: 34-35) The language "laying at the apostles feet" indicates that the one selling the property is yielding to the authority of the apostles and showing respect for the manner in which the apostles will distribute the money.[5] Respecting the authority of the leaders of this fledgling community will be an essential component of growing the early church. Not only do these believers exhibit a changed view on the purpose of their wealth, but they are willing to entrust the distribution of their wealth to their leaders. Their eyes have moved off of themselves as their priority has shifted to expanding the gospel and caring for God's people.

Dr. Luke, the writer of Acts and a writer with a very keen eye for detail, nestles two important verses in between his explanation of the community's approach to sharing and his account of Ananias and Sapphira. In verses 36-37 of chapter 4 we read of how Joseph, whom the apostles have nicknamed Barnabas, sells some land and gives the proceeds to the apostles. Why does Luke give this specific example? Many others have done the very same thing; why single out this particular transaction? As we look at these verses together, I think we will see just how much Ananias and Sapphira were seeking the approval of the apostles as well as increased stature within their community.

In your own community, how often do you notice desperation in those around you as people climb over one another to get ahead? How has the teen-girl phenomenon of the "queen bee" seemed to have spread to the adults you know?

Joseph was a Jew, from the tribe of Levi, meaning that his family's inheritance was working in the temple. Fourteen to fifteen hundred years prior, when the Israelites crossed into their Promised Land, each tribe from the 12 sons of Jacob were given an inheritance of land. All except for the sons of Levi, that is. The Levites had been the only ones to stand with Moses after Aaron led the Israelites in forming a golden calf for them to worship. As a result of their standing with Moses and choosing God, God rewarded them with an inheritance of service in His holy temple. Levites were responsible for serving the Lord and only they could work in the temple as priests, musicians, temple workers, and even as distributors of the tithe. Joseph, a Levite, was born on the island of Cyprus, but is at this time living in Jerusalem. He is known and loved by the apostles who have nicknamed him "Barnabas", which is probably derived from the Aramaic expression *bar* (son of) and *nabi* (prophet) and would be translated as "son of Exhortation". [6] It is obvious from his very name that the apostles recognized in Barnabas his great gifting as a preacher.

Imagine with me where we are in church history. These are very early days. Christ has ascended. Pentecost has occurred. Peter has preached a few good sermons. The early believers are depending on one another for support. The church has NOT gone beyond the boundaries of Jerusalem. Real structure has NOT yet been put into place in the church in Jerusalem. Saul has NOT yet been converted. Persecution has NOT yet begun. In order for this movement of God to expand and survive the coming persecution, the people of God will not only need to be unified, but there will need to be preachers who will GO and share the gospel beyond the walls of Jerusalem.

The apostles see in Barnabas a man who is highly gifted at preaching and exhortation—encouraging others to commendable conduct. Barnabas will be one of the first of the Jerusalem leaders to believe in the authenticity of Saul's conversion and will take it in hand to introduce him to the apostles. When believers begin to flee Jerusalem because of persecution, the apostles will send Barnabas to their aid in Antioch. It will be Barnabas who will go to Tarsus in search of Saul to bring him back to Antioch where together they will preach for an entire year, growing the church by leaps and bounds. It is at this time and in this place that believers were first called "Christians". We don't know it yet in the 4th chapter of Acts, but Barnabas will ultimately become the prophet and teacher who will accompany Paul on his first missionary journey. Doesn't Barnabas sound like an amazing person and young leader to you?

We don't know why Barnabas sold his plot of land. Perhaps he felt God's tug on his heart to travel light. Perhaps he sensed that some would need to be willing to GO and spread the gospel and his heart was willing so he didn't want to be tied down. Perhaps someone simply had a need and he answered the call. As the apostles accept the proceeds from the sale of Barnabas' land, you get a sense that the apostles were not the only ones who recognized great giftedness in Barnabas. Ananias and Sapphira no doubt stood by and watched, and imagined a vain thing.

How do you feel when someone else displays a talent or enjoys a success you can only dream about? Does your own insufficiency leave you feeling small or insecure? Threatened or vulnerable? Challenged to push harder? Can you rejoice in someone else's success? Please take some time to be transparent here.

If you're truly honest, how often do you look at someone else's spiritual gifts with envy, wishing that you had their gifting and feeling like you somehow don't measure up because of how God has gifted you?

In his beautiful chapter on the importance of *all* the spiritual gifts, Paul reminds us in 1 Corinthians 12 that all of the members of the body of Christ have a gifting and a purpose that is uniquely their own and intentionally given by God. Paul tells us in verse 18 "God has placed the members, each one of them, in the body, just as He desired." Do you see yourself as a smelly foot when you would rather be a nimble hand? Scant eyelashes when you would rather be the powerful eye itself? God has equipped you exactly as He has seen fit for the work He has purposed for you to do. And He does have specific work for you to do in His kingdom! In order to do all He has called us to do for Him, we must rely on the gifts He has given to us. Our sense of identity and worthiness should never come from how we feel about *what we do* but must come from *who we are* in Christ. We are to be content with the giftedness God has given us and not always be comparing ourselves to other people and yearning for their gifts. Do not undervalue the gifts that God has given to you!

Ananias and Sapphira had much to be thankful for. They were members of the new community of believers. They had one another. They had wealth enough to sell a piece of land and not be destitute themselves. But it was still not enough. They saw the respect and position that Barnabas held within the community and they envied him. They wanted what he had without giving what he gave.

Every community places value on that which it esteems most highly. In some communities it may be wealth, corporate success, or academic credentials. In another it may be athleticism, wit, or social connectedness. And in yet another it may be honesty, integrity, and love. Whatever the case, when our identity is marked by a desire to rise to the top of our social group, we will be plagued by constant fears of not measuring up, tiresome jealousies, and feelings of inferiority.

In the community/communities you are a part of, what things are most highly valued? How do you feel you rank in these areas?

If you are honest, how often do you yearn or strive to be held in higher esteem within your community?

Ananias and Sapphira knew Barnabas. They worshipped with him. Like everyone else, they knew of his devotion to the Lord. Barnabas "was a good man, full of the Holy Spirit and of faith. And considerable numbers were brought to the Lord" through him. (Acts 11:24) They saw what he had and they became desperately jealous. What exactly did they want? Was it his gifting as a teacher? Perhaps. We have all experienced times when we look at our own gifting with disdain, craving someone else's gifts and talents instead. Or perhaps they were simply indignant that an outsider, a Cypriot, could rise to a place of such esteem while they felt so insignificant. Either way, they allowed jealousy to consume them as they took their eyes off Christ as the source of their identity and placed it in their position within their community instead.

And so Ananias and Sapphira, following on the heels of Barnabas, sell their own piece of land, and present an offering of the proceeds to the apostles. Beforehand however, the couple has conspired together to retain some of the proceeds for themselves, all the while claiming to be giving everything to the work of the Lord.

So, they wanted to keep a little of the money for themselves. Is that really such a bad thing? Does having money go against God's wishes for us? Verses such as: "for the love of money is a root of all sorts of evil" (1 Timothy 6:10) and "it is easier for a camel to go through the eye of a needle, than for a rich man to enter the kingdom of God" (Matthew 19:24) might lead us to believe that God is against His followers having wealth. But scripture is loaded with examples of individuals who had riches and chose to use them for God's work. Think of Lydia in the New Testament. We know she was wealthy because she was a seller of purple fabric, which was a very expensive product in the first century, and because her home was large enough for the entire congregation of the first church in Philippi to meet there. Lydia used her wealth to serve the Lord. Think about the Proverbs 31 Woman from Chapter 1. She too had great wealth—she had servants, land, businesses—and is in no way criticized by God for her wealth. Both women had great wealth; both used their money for the Lord's work. Many other figures in the Bible were exceedingly wealthy, such as Abraham, Isaac, Jacob, David, and Solomon. Money is a gift, like any other, that comes directly from God, and should always be held loosely for Him to use it as He purposes.

Why do we want money so badly and why does it seem we are never content with the amount we have? Everyone wants and needs money to have the things that money can buy, but many people crave the status that accompanies those things. Status in today's world means power, and power is exactly what Ananias and Sapphira wanted. Have you ever noticed how people of means are seen as more important than those who have much less? To be seen as one of the wealthiest leaders in the community would immediately make them feel more important. So often the danger with having a lot of money is that it leads us to prideful thoughts and attitudes. When I close my eyes and think of myself, I want to see Christ, and not my wealth or physical appearance or career or my own status and power within my community.

How does your personal financial situation influence the way you feel about your position in your community?

Do you think having more money would elevate your position within your community?

Oftentimes we can deceive ourselves by saying that we want more money so we can be more generous with others and ultimately serve God better. In our self-deceit we don't realize that rather than wanting to serve others, we really just want to be *recognized* for serving others. Have you ever thought something like this, "Lord, if I had this vacation home, think how I could serve you more by inviting believers to come here to be refreshed"? Or how about this one, "Lord, if I could only have that promotion at work, I could earn so much more money to put into circulation in your kingdom work"? We are wading into very dangerous territory here when we begin to bargain with God about how we could help Him out, if only He would bless us a little more financially. Practice generosity when you have little, or you will be unlikely to give generously when you have more.

We can also yearn for more money because we are desperately afraid of "not having enough". Are we really afraid of poverty? In some instances—such as long-term unemployment or under-employment, or a chronic health condition that depletes all of our savings, or an accident or natural disaster that wipes out everything we own—the risk of poverty may be a real possibility. But in most cases, our fear of "not having enough" is a fear fueled by our tendency to compare ourselves to others and to what they have, and to desperately want to keep up. We have to relinquish this yearning to have it all and practice trusting His promise that "God shall supply all your needs according to His riches in glory in Christ Jesus." (Philippians 4:19)

Underlying the fear of "not having enough" is a real doubt that God will provide for *all* of our needs. God doesn't promise to give us everything we want, but He does promise to supply all our needs. What we find as we walk more and more closely with Him is that our list of perceived needs tends to diminish the more we rely on Him. The more we read of His promises to us in His word, the more we begin to understand His nature and His overwhelming love for us. As we begin to grasp some measure of His love for us, we can begin to let go of some of our fears of not having enough. And as we see Him provide for our needs, we learn to trust in Him more.

What does the fact that Ananias and Sapphira held back some of the proceeds for themselves reveal about their faith in God and in His provision toward them personally?

How do you act similarly today by telling "small" lies or embellishing your story to make yourself look better as you compete within your own social network?

The lie that they had given everything to the work of the Lord was fueled by their pride and desire to be perceived in the same light as Barnabas. Solomon warns us in Proverbs 16: 18 that "pride goes before destruction, and a haughty spirit before stumbling." It's too bad Ananias and Sapphira didn't remember that verse! Undoubtedly inspired by the Holy Spirit, Peter sees right through their lies and what they have done and reminds Ananias that he was under absolutely no compulsion to sell his land and give the proceeds to the church. In what seems a shockingly harsh punishment, Ananias is immediately struck dead. Where was Sapphira during this time? Why did no one tell her of her husband's death? Did Peter summon her, instructing the messengers to say nothing of Ananias' untimely death in order to see how Sapphira would respond to his questions of her? We don't know the answers to these questions, but not more than 3 hours after the death of her husband, Sapphira arrives and Peter asks her to confirm how much money they received from the sale of their land. Upon confirming the amount that Peter uttered, Sapphira too fell down dead.

What are these drastic punishments from the hand of a loving God all about anyway? Is this really the best way to launch the early Christian church? Perhaps yes. Perhaps it was the only way. When we read this account we can't help but see the similarity with the story of Achan in Joshua 6-7. In that account, the children of Israel had just crossed over the Jordan River on their journey to their "Promised Land". Claiming the city of Jericho would be their first battle in settling into their Promised Land. They were under strict orders to take none of the spoils for themselves; everything was to be dedicated to the Lord. One man, Achan, disobeyed these orders and kept some of the spoils for himself, hiding them in his tent. Did he also lack faith in God's provision for him personally? Was he hoping additional wealth might somehow elevate him in his community? The Lord revealed to Joshua that it was Achan who had sinned and so he, his entire family, all of his possessions, and the spoils he had stolen were all burned up by fire. Heavy punishment. But perhaps not an unjust one.

Throughout scripture, the "Promised Land" refers not only to the physical place to which God guided the children of Israel, but also to the metaphorical condition He has for us when we are living our life under the guidance of the Holy Spirit, doing the will of the Father, and enjoying sweet fellowship with the Son. When we are fulfilling the purposes for which He created us, we are truly living in our Promised Land, a foretaste of God's kingdom here on earth. Don't you see how this is no place for outright sin, lack of faith in God's provision, and perhaps most importantly, a desire to place anything other than God Himself at the center of our life?

Even as the Israelites were moving into new territory as they claimed their Promised Land, so the early church would be claiming new territory as it moved out of Jerusalem, spreading the gospel to Judea, and Samaria, and the uttermost ends of the earth. The people had to be pure for God to be fully at work in and through them. Deceit could not be tolerated; unity was essential. Knowing this to be true, the final great prayer that Jesus offered to the Father before going to the cross was for the unity of all the believers who would follow after Him. "I do not ask in behalf of these alone, but for those also who believe in Me through their word; that they may all be one; even as Thou, Father, art in Me, and I in Thee, that they also may be in Us; that the world may believe that Thou didst send Me." (John 17:20-21) In order for the gospel to spread and take root, these early believers had to be united, full of integrity, and fully convinced of the all-sufficiency of the Lord Jesus for meeting all of their needs.

Just before Peter pronounces God's judgment on Ananias, he asks him why he has allowed Satan to so fill his heart. He goes on to say that he has lied to the Holy Spirit of God. Peter also tells Sapphira that she has tested the Spirit of the Lord. Clearly there is a spiritual battle going on here. When we are undergoing feelings of inadequacy, jealousy toward another individual, or yearnings for things we don't have, Satan is all too eager to get involved in the battle that is raging within our spirit. Peter himself warns us in 1 Peter 5:8 to "be on the alert (because) your adversary, the devil, prowls about like a roaring lion, seeking someone to devour." We will look more closely at the role of Satan in our battles with our identity in Chapter 9.

What we are yearning for has a name and it is called Popularity. That elusive quality that makes some people the coolest, most dynamic, most likely to be followed member of their group. Whether it's based on real, tangible qualities or just a vibe someone gives off, we want it because we think it will fill an empty place. The empty place that whispers in the dark, "if I'm popular, then I'll be okay."

Galinda in the Broadway hit musical "Wicked" explains it this way:

"When I see depressing creatures,
With unprepossessing features,
I remind them on their own behalf

To think of
Celebrated heads of state,
Or 'specially great communicators!
Did they have brains or knowledge?
Don't make me laugh!

They were POPULAR!
Please!
It's all about popular.
It's not about aptitude,
It's the way you're viewed,
So it's very shrewd to be,
Very very popular
like ME!"[7]

How are you trying to gain the approval and acceptance of those around you? Do you make sure you are doing *exactly* what everyone else is doing—including your activities and those of your children: sports, camps, clubs, vacations—just to be sure you are keeping up?

How important is it to you that others know what you have accomplished or done? That they know *what* or *who* you know? Must you be the first one to give a movie, restaurant, or vacation review to your friends to be the one "in the know"? Do you name drop?

When we are in a social setting, it is so easy to look around us and waste our time comparing ourselves to everyone else and to focus our energy on self-promotion. That is what we tend to observe in others, isn't it? Even in Christian circles there can be a real competition to be the first one to reference a particular Bible verse or to be the one with the most eloquent prayer. Whether in secular groups or Christian, we behave like a "social climber" when our identity is rooted in how that group perceives us rather than in how God sees us. When our own position or sense of power in a group is overly important to us, our speech will reveal that we are self-focused rather than others-focused.

Do you feel you are attentive to what *someone else* is telling you in conversation and ask questions to learn more *about them,* or do you often look for ways to turn the conversation back to you to talk about something *you* have done?

Proverbs 12:23 cautions: "Prudent people don't flaunt their knowledge; talkative fools broadcast their silliness." (MSG) And Proverbs 14:3 is even more blunt: "Proud fools talk too much!" (Good News Translation) How is listening and not always talking important for you to practice when you struggle with needing to be popular?

Frequent bragging about my own accomplishments reveals a deep insecurity in my own heart about who I am. Constantly needing to top someone's story with something I have done highlights the empty places in my own heart that I am trying to fill with others' acceptance and admiration of me. God wants to fill all of the empty places in our hearts! He is the Alpha and the Omega, the beginning and the end and everything in between. He is El-Shaddai, the All-Sufficient God and He is to be *enough* for us. He is to be our sufficiency.

The Lord is gently revealing himself as El-Shaddai to a dear friend of mine who, like many of us, struggles with feelings of insecurity. In His deep love for her, He has begun to reveal to her how often in her speech she repeats what has been said, simply to hear herself talk. Don't we all love to hear ourselves talk? She calls it "mimicking" and is asking God to help her see when she is tempted to mimic. She knows God wants to set her free from the trap of setting her identity in how she is perceived by a group. The message God has been telling my friend is true for you as well: "don't keep trying to prove your worth by what you say, I proved your worth when I died for you."

When you catch yourself talking, bragging, or "story topping" too much, how can you identify the empty place in your heart that you are trying to fill with others' respect for you?

How frequently do you try to prove your own self worth and thereby increase your own popularity by bragging about the accomplishments of your children?

Sapphira longed for respect and admiration from within her social group. She longed to be viewed as the most generous because generosity was a highly valued quality in her community. She saw the esteem that someone else had and decided she would do anything to attain that same level of esteem—even if that meant lying and cheating to get there. There was a vast empty place deep within Sapphira's heart, a place that cried out for significance and importance, and rather than allowing the deep, deep love of God for her to fill that void, she tried to fill it on her own terms. She failed to recognize that her significance rested in her being cherished by the Father and redeemed by the Son.

God is always most concerned about the condition of our heart. He made you for a purpose, with your own particular gifts and talents to accomplish everything He has imagined for you. Paul reminds us in Ephesians 2:10 that "we are His workmanship, created in Christ Jesus for good works, which God prepared *beforehand* (emphasis mine) that we should walk in them." Our source of all strength must come from Him. As soon as we start looking anywhere else for our source of strength, joy, and identity, we will be headed for trouble, just as Ananias and Sapphira were. In a little twist of irony, Ananias' name means "God is merciful" and Sapphira means "beautiful"[8]. This is a simple reminder that God, in His mercy, has beautifully made each of us exactly as He intended. Our challenge in a fallen and broken world is to keep our eyes on Him, the all-sufficient One, as the source of our identity, so that we may become all that He has intended for us to be.

As you respond in worship to what God is showing you, please listen to "My Desire" by Jeremy Camp on the "Restored" album. Will you lay down your desire to be someone someday? Will you give God your need to have purpose inside and ask Him to make your purpose to do His will? Will you declare, "My desire is to be used by You"?

7

Sarah and The Woman with the Hemorrhage – My Identity is in My Health

Genesis 18:1-15
Mark 5:25-34
Luke 8:43-48
Matthew 9:20-22

Does it ever seem to you that some families are always suffering from one health crisis after another while other families can go entire years without ever once pulling out their medical insurance cards? Even within a family there often seems to be one person who gets more than his or her fair share of illness. For these individuals and families, a day without aches, pains and worries is a welcome respite in a life that is overshadowed by illness.

What are some words that you would use to describe your physical body? Tall? Short? Heavy? Thin? Sickly? Strong? Damaged? Abused? Energetic? Healthy? Tired? Broken? Addicted?

Do you suffer from a chronic disorder or a long-standing addiction? Are your days punctuated by chronic pain, migraines, joint or bone pain, or old injuries? Describe how it feels to be one who is always unwell. (Use your imagination if you are one who is blessed with good health.)

My family is one of those families that seem to excel at giving our health care providers challenges in the diagnostic department! We never seem to get a break when it comes to medical issues. Here are a few of the choice quotes, as best as I can recall them, from some of the doctors I have met over the years:

"You don't usually see shingles in a 5 year old."
"This is the worst cavity in a clean mouth that I have seen in 20 years. The bone of one tooth has fused with the root of the tooth next to it."
"This is among the rarest forms of cancer; only about 25 people in the world have it."
"Very rarely does enamel not form on a child's teeth; this causes them to decay and crumble."
"We have to do an MRI to determine why your 2 year old suddenly can't walk—is it cellulitis or septic arthritis?"
"Children don't usually die being diagnosed with diabetes."
Even the dog gets in on the act: "I've heard about being allergic to the dissolution of the stitches, but in 25 years of veterinary practice, I've never seen it, until now."

I guess I should be happy that I am helping my medical professionals hone their diagnostic skills! But sometimes I just want to shout, "Enough!"

And these are just the biggies. Add to them the broken bones, the dislocated shoulders, the chronic ear infections in one child for 5 years, or the 5 cases of Lyme disease in 3 children in 3 years! In fact, the very day I had planned to start writing this chapter, my daughter, who is in high school, came down with a case of head lice! I'm not kidding! My entire day was derailed as I spent 4 ½ hours combing out her beautiful, thick, waist-length hair. The response I heard over and over again was, "high school kids don't usually get lice; that's something little kids get." There we go again—experiencing the unusual when it comes to anything medical! Expressions like "being a nit-picker" and "going over something with a fine tooth comb" take on a whole new meaning for me now! Do you understand why I feel I should have a Frequent Flyer Card at my local pediatrician's office?

Whether it's a series of medical crises one after the other or a chronic disorder that offers no relief-even for a few days at a time-it can be overwhelming to be constantly tried and tested in matters of one's health. It can be very difficult to carry on trusting God and to see oneself as He sees us, rather than as an unhealthy, broken individual.

Have you ever had a season of your life when you or your family was buffeted again and again by medical problems or by one big crisis? If so, please describe how this felt.

Do you feel like there is a certain stigma or pity attached to you or your family because of a chronic illness? How does this feel?

If you get very quiet and honest before God, do you feel like His allowing you to be sick reveals that He loves you less than someone who is healthy? Conversely, do you feel like your good health is a reward for your love for Him and your obedience to Him? Be honest.

When we, or someone in our family, suffer from chronic health issues, we can go one of two ways: either we can let it define us, or we can find our identity in God in spite of our circumstances. Many individuals in the Bible suffer from physical infirmities. Two such women, Sarah in the Old Testament, and the woman with the hemorrhage in the New Testament, respond very differently to how they allow their infirmities to shape their identity. Sarah, the wife of Abraham, allows her barrenness to define her, whereas the woman who touched Jesus' hem refused to be identified by her bleeding condition.

Beginning when Abraham was 75 and Sarah was 65, God repeatedly promises Abraham that he would be the 'father of many nations" and would have descendants too numerous to count. (See Genesis 12:2, 13:16, 15:4-5, 17:2-7.) There is only one problem, and we've seen it before in the Old Testament, specifically in this family: Sarah is barren. Ten years after God first promises them many descendants, they are still childless. Sarah decides she has waited long enough and gives Abraham her Egyptian handmaid, Hagar, to bear a child for her. Sarah lets us know her view of things: "The LORD has prevented me from bearing children." (Genesis 16:2) I think I hear shades of Eve's blame game in her tone, don't you? Sarah will quickly regret giving her maid to her husband as Hagar's pregnancy leads her to act disrespectfully toward her mistress.

When God institutes the covenant of circumcision in Genesis 17, He has one final word for Abraham. Sarah, who is by this time 89, will have a son. This is the first time God specifically says that *Sarah* will be the mother of the child through whom His covenant with Abraham will pass. (Genesis 17:19) Even Abraham is by this point too old to father a child, so a child from the union of Sarah and Abraham would be nothing short of a miracle from God. And yet, the Lord promises him one more son, the child of the promise.

As the 18ᵗʰ chapter of Genesis opens, we find Abraham and Sarah at home in their tents by the oak grove at Mamre. Abraham is 99 years old and Sarah is 89.

Please read the passage from Genesis 18. Write down everything you notice about how Abraham treated the three men. How did he address them? What did he do?

___

Abraham immediately recognizes that these men are worthy of respect and honor. He invites them to linger awhile with him as he rushes to have a fine meal prepared for them. Calling them "Adonai" or "lord", meaning "master", he is giving them a place of authority over his life. As the meal is winding down, they inquire for the first time about Sarah.

Where is Sarah?

___

What promise is made of Sarah?

___

How does Sarah respond to this promise?

___

Sarah didn't believe it was possible for her to bear a child at her advanced age, and so she laughs. I don't believe this was a simple laugh of astonishment at the news, but rather a mocking laughter indicative of a strong disbelief in the possibility of God doing this type of miracle in her. Look at Genesis 17:17. Abraham also laughed when he was told Sarah would have a son, but the Lord does not reprimand him for laughing. Why not? I don't think Abraham didn't believe God *could* do such a thing; I think he simply wondered why God *would* do such a thing when he already had a son. Abraham wanted the promises to go through his 13-year old son, Ishmael, whom he dearly loves.

We see a similar pattern in the book of Luke when the angel Gabriel visits both Zacharias (the father of John the Baptist) and Mary within a span of a few months, telling them both that they will have a son. Zacharias asks, "How will I know this for certain? I am an old man and my wife is advanced in years," and is punished for his doubt by being made mute until John's birth. Mary asks God, "How can this be since I am a virgin?" and is not punished. Did doubt lace both of these questions? Probably not. Our all-knowing, always-just God looks at the heart, not just the outward display. In Zacharias He saw doubt and a need for a sign; in Mary He saw surprise and wonder at God's plan.

Likewise in Genesis, God sees in Abraham the heart of a father longing for the promises to pass through his son Ishmael, whereas in Sarah, He sees doubt and mocking at the plan of God. Sarah's laughter is her way of declaring to God, "you can't do something that big!" Sarah's "I am" statements might look something like this: "I am barren." "I am old." "I am fruitless." "I am not, and never will be, a mother." Her barrenness had gone on for too long—she was hopeless. When we allow our present situation to become our identity, it is very difficult to believe that God is powerful enough to change us.

Sarah not only heard the promise and chose to disbelieve, she lied about having laughed in order to protect herself. Our enemy, the father of lies, wants nothing more than to have us believe ugly lies about ourselves so that we are rendered less effective in God's kingdom. When we are consumed by a false identity it becomes all too easy to listen to those lies and to repeat them to ourselves and to God in bitterness or self-defeat. But to have a whole and healthy relationship with Him, we must be truthful with Him at all times, even when it's painful to do so. The Lord God "desires truth in the innermost being." (Psalm 51:6) Sarah had an opportunity to confess that she had lied, but she was so steeped in her identity as a barren woman that she couldn't be honest, even when she was confronted.

Because barrenness had become Sarah's identity, she didn't believe God could work in her, she lied about her disbelief, and most sad of all, she distanced herself from God.

Where is Sarah throughout the entire story?

Reread verses 9-13 carefully. Who is really talking with Abraham?

The absolutely astonishing thing we read in verse 13 is that this is Jehovah, the LORD, who is speaking with Abraham! Many Bible scholars believe that this is one of the Old Testament appearances of the pre-incarnate Christ who is speaking with Abraham, along with two angels. You will see in Genesis 18:16, 18:22, and 19:1 that the two angels carry on to the city of Sodom, while the LORD stays behind to talk with Abraham. Other scholars assert that this is a representation of the Trinity in bodily form. In either case, one thing is certain: it is the LORD God who has come to Abraham and Sarah's home. Please don't miss this. *God himself is sitting under her oak trees and Sarah won't go out of the tent!* God was right there and she stayed where she was. Don't do this, friends. When God wants to be there with us in our trials, don't stay in your tent! Use the trial you are suffering as an opportunity to move toward God in faith. As God Himself says to Abraham in verse 14, "Is anything to difficult for the LORD?" When we have an unhealthy view of ourselves, it becomes all too easy to hide in our tent, away from others and away from God, lost in the self-pity of a broken identity. I know—feelings of despair, hidden sorrow, shame, and depression can become overwhelming at times. But our infirmities, when turned over to God, can be opportunities to allow His power to work through us. In a beautiful passage in 2 Corinthians 12:7-11, Paul tells us how he relies on God's grace to carry him through his own afflictions and he concludes, "when I am weak, then I am strong." God wants us to find our strength in Him, not in ourselves and in our own capabilities.

Sarah was barren a long time before the Lord finally decided to answer her prayer for a child. We learn of her barrenness when she is 65, but remember, living in an ancient culture, she has probably felt the sting of being barren since she was a 15-year old young married woman. That's a long time to suffer a chronic disorder. When we suffer from a chronic disease or ailment for a long time, it is so easy to see ourselves through the lens of that disease. It is important to remember that that's not how God sees us. He sees us as His dearly loved children (Ephesians 5:1), fearfully and wonderfully made (Psalm 139:14), beautiful (throughout the Song of Solomon), and the apple of His eye (Zechariah 2:8). Regardless of the physical state of your body, when you are in Christ, your body is the temple (or dwelling place) of the Holy Spirit. (1 Corinthians 6:19) This is how He sees you.

How can a lack of health lead us to bitterness and ultimately separation from God?

When we define ourselves by the state of our physical health, we will tend to move away from our relationship with God rather than moving toward Him. We will doubt His promises to us, like Sarah did. We will believe the lies about ourselves and even repeat them to God. And we will separate ourselves from fellowship with God like Sarah did when she hid in the tent. Sarah's story does not have to be our story. When our identity is rooted in God regardless of our health, we will move forward in faith with a healthy, honest view of ourselves, all the while keeping our eyes on Christ, not on ourselves and on our problems.

The woman in the gospels referred to simply as "the woman with the hemorrhage" is someone who, though sick for an extended period of time, does not allow her infirmity to become her identity. We can learn much from looking into her life.

The 24 hours before we meet the woman with the hemorrhage are very busy ones for Jesus. We find him crossing the Sea of Galilee, calming the raging wind and sea, healing a man possessed by many demons, casting the demons into a herd of swine that promptly run over the cliffs to be drowned in the sea, and then He crosses back over to the other side of the Sea of Galilee. Up all night, at work all day, He must have returned exhausted and in need of a little quiet time! Can you relate? What He finds when He gets to the other side is that a crowd of people is already there, waiting for Him, longing for a word or a touch from Him. And so Jesus, in His compassion, lingers by the seashore with the crowd that is so eager to approach Him.

She must have heard He was there. Perhaps she saw Him get in the boat and cross to the other side and decided to await His return. Perhaps she heard the crowd gathering and decided this was her moment. But before she could approach Jesus, someone else, someone more important, got to Him first.

Jairus was his name. Jairus, one of the few synagogue officials who actually would ask for Jesus' help. Surely his needs are much more important to Jesus than healing an unknown woman of an unknown disorder that has caused her to bleed constantly for 12 years. Jairus' little

119

daughter is only 12 years old after all, and if Jesus doesn't come quickly, she will die. Twelve years—such a short time if it's a life that ends too quickly; such a long time if you're sick during all those years.

When illness seems to cling to you like a wet blanket, does it seem like everyone else around you is healthy and somehow more important to God than you?

Moved by compassion, Jesus sets out with Jairus, leaving the seashore to go to Jairus' house to heal his daughter. What about the crowd? Would they just disburse after waiting such a long time for Jesus to arrive? Not a chance! They are not about to let Him go now. Some of the words used to describe this throng of people are: multitude, following, crowding, pressing in. This is not a single-file line proceeding in an orderly fashion to Jairus' house. This is a desperate crowd, all wanting something from Jesus—a touch, a word, a healing, a promise of a better future.

Where do you go when you have a desperate need? To the mall? To the refrigerator? To self-pity? To a friend? To God? Be honest and describe your typical responses.

She had a desperate need. She went to many physicians. She spent all she had. She was made worse, not better. I don't even want to imagine what experimental treatments she had done to her over these 12 years that made her worse. I'm sure this wasn't pills and potions, but rather, painful ancient procedures in an age before the practices of modern medicine. Can you imagine with me how tired she was from struggling against this disease for all these years? She must have felt overwhelmed and hopeless at times as it appeared there was no end in sight to her dreadful condition. She had endured all that physicians could do for her and she was still in desperate need. She needed the touch of the Great Physician.

Imagine what it must be like to suffer from an illness for 12 years. How would this form your view of yourself?

Unlike Sarah, the woman with the hemorrhage believed she could be healed. Even though she had been bleeding continuously for 12 years, she still believed Jesus could heal her if she could just get close enough to touch Him. Her infirmity had not become her identity.

But how could she, an "unclean" woman, receive a touch from the Great Physician? According to the Law of Moses, her bleeding condition rendered her "unclean" and as such she had to separate herself from the community. God had given the ancient Hebrews very strict laws regarding what was ceremonially clean and what was unclean. As we have seen before, God has always desired to dwell among or tabernacle with His people. The Law of Moses is chiefly concerned with how an unholy people can worship God in His holy tabernacle. Leviticus 11:44, "Be holy for I am holy", is really the cornerstone of the entire Law. The Christian Leadership Center describes uncleanness this way:

"God's people had to learn that God is so holy, so separated from the physical, so distinct from this corrupted world, that everything in His presence must be sanctified by atonement. Whatever Leviticus calls unclean is simply not compatible with God's holiness. The term "unclean" may describe sin, sickness, bodily discharges, mildew on the wall, corruption and defilement; it describes what is not in its pristine condition, what is abnormal, unhealthy, weakened, or contaminated. It does not always describe sinfulness."[9]

The specific law telling her she is unclean is found in Leviticus 15:25. "Now if a woman has a discharge of her blood many days, not at the period of her menstrual impurity, or if she has a discharge beyond that period, all the days of her impure discharge she shall continue as though in her menstrual impurity; she is unclean." Twelve years. For four thousand three hundred eighty days she has been unclean. As long as she was unclean, she would be separated from others as her defilement would be communicated to everything with which she would come in contact. During the time the Temple existed, it was typical for a "niddah" (the name for a menstruating woman during the period of her uncleanness) to be completely segregated from the community, staying in a special dwelling known as a "house for uncleanness".[10]

Can you just imagine? She was all alone. An outcast. No companionship. No touch. No opportunity to go to the Temple to worship. Her heart must have echoed the words of King Hezekiah in Psalm 42 when his illness made him unclean and unable to go to the Temple to worship: "As the deer pants for the water brooks, so my soul pants for Thee, O God. My soul thirsts for God, for the living God; when shall I come and appear before God?"

Describe a time when you felt you were in a hopeless situation and cried out, "Why me? What did I do to deserve this?"

How do you prevent despair from becoming anger and bitterness against God?

On any day when there was less blood than usual, she must have had false hope that her condition was improving, only to have those hopes dashed when the flow returned to normal. As she "endured much at the hands of many physicians", she must have thought, "I'll be willing to undergo *this treatment* if only it would *guarantee* I'll get better." We all need a little hope, don't we? I think not knowing if things will ever improve and the fear that things could even get worse is the hardest aspect of dealing with chronic illness.

Have you ever experienced these feelings of despair? Please describe.

Remarkably, this unclean woman shakes off any feelings of despair and boldly pushes through the crowd, *defiling everyone she touches*. It's now or never. When God is driving you to Himself, don't delay. Go to Him. Whether He's drawing you to trust in Him for the first time, or if He's calling you to go deeper with Him in daily prayer and Bible study, answer His call. No matter our condition—who we are, what we've done, or how we see ourselves—He always invites us to reach out and touch Him.

And so she touches Him. Or rather, the hem of His garments—even though she risks defiling Him—and is immediately made well. Can you imagine her joy? Can you imagine her surprise when her flow stopped *immediately*? Can you feel her joy turn to terror as Jesus asks who touched

Him? She knows that everyone in the crowd—including Jesus—has the right to be outraged that she, an unclean woman, has appeared before them and touched so many of them. The woman who has been in isolation for 12 years must have wanted to run home and hide! I suppose like Sarah, she could have lied and said she didn't touch Jesus. But her "I am" statement was not "I am unclean". Her "I am" statement was: "I am a woman in need of a touch from Jesus". She believed Jesus could heal her, even though she had suffered for such a long time, and so she boldly and honestly presented herself before Him. She was more focused on what Jesus could do in her life than she was on the physical condition of her life. To live with an identity rooted in God, regardless of our health, we need to keep our eyes on Jesus and believe that nothing is impossible for God.

How can you make her "I am" statement your "I am" statement: "I am a woman in need of a touch from Jesus"?

What if we don't have any major health concerns? Can our identity still be mistakenly rooted in our physical health? Absolutely. If we are not careful, we can unwittingly get caught up in thinking that our good health is due to our righteous behavior and that as long as we do things that are pleasing to God, He will protect us. This "if…then" mentality is really just modern day legalism and we should be on guard against it.

Growing up in a Christian home and loving God deeply from a young age, I never thought I had any issues with conditional love for God. I loved Him, and my life was fairly disease and pain-free. I didn't think I was correlating these two facts, but somewhere down deep, I was. When my son was diagnosed with type 1 diabetes at age 5, I became deeply angry and disappointed at God. This was the same disease that took the life of my brother when he was only 8 years old and has afflicted my sister since she was 16. We had just come off a particularly difficult season of health problems that spanned a 5-year period and we were moving state the following week. I was exhausted and I couldn't handle one more disease. Certainly not this disease. As God worked through much healing in my own heart, I became painfully aware that lurking there in the depths of my heart was an underlying notion that if I behaved like a "good Christian girl" then surely He would protect me. "Didn't He owe me that much?" I whispered.

His question to me was almost audible: "Bonnie, do you trust that I am good even when everything around you would say otherwise?" In His mercy He has shown me that He is good all the time, even when times are not so good in my life.

If you are fortunate enough not to have any major health concerns of your own, how can you guard against feeling that your "righteousness" has somehow bought you that protection from God?"

Where do we go with our faith when, unlike Sarah and the woman with the hemorrhage, He chooses *not* to heal? First, never stop going out of the tent! Do not let your infirmity separate you from the love of God. Keep meeting with Him. James 1:2-4 and Romans 5:3-5 remind us that when we undergo trials (including physical ailments) we are given an opportunity to strengthen our faith by persevering. Choose to believe in the God who is *"able* to deliver you...even if He *does not"*. (Daniel 3:17-18) Even Paul, who suffered beatings, imprisonment, and shipwrecks, as well as a condition from which God did not heal him in this life, had this to say about our physical condition: "though our outer man is decaying, yet our inner man is being renewed day by day. For momentary, light affliction is producing for us an eternal weight of glory far beyond all comparison." (2 Corinthians 4: 16-17) Let Him renew your inner person day by day.

Secondly, trust that God will redeem your situation. In the Bible, "to redeem" means not only "to repurchase what was sold", but also "to rescue from captivity", "to recover", "to make amends for".[11] This means that God can work through and bring blessing out of what appears to be a lost situation. God is in the redeeming business! Look at the mess Abraham and Sarah made in giving Hagar to Abraham. And yet, even through all that mess, God redeems their situation by bringing blessing on Hagar and Ishmael as He promises that even Ishmael would be the father of multitudes. It is when we stop believing that God can work through our infirmity that the illness itself becomes our identity. Trust God's promise in Joel 2:25 when He says that He "will make up to you for the years that the swarming locust has eaten." Years spent suffering from illness do not have to be wasted years in God's economy.

And finally, remember that His eye is always on you and Jesus is always interceding for you, even when He is not healing you. I have long known Romans 8:34 which says that Jesus "is at the right hand of God, who also intercedes for us", but recently a fresh reading of Mark 6 drew for me a clearer picture of Jesus' prayer-life on our behalf. The chapter begins with Jesus sending out the twelve apostles to preach and heal in the neighboring towns. While they are gone, John the Baptist, Jesus' cousin, is beheaded. When the apostles return, they have much they want to share with one another, but they continue to be interrupted by those who want a touch from Jesus.

Jesus suggests they get away by boat to a lonely place to rest awhile, but before they could reach the shore, the crowd has raced ahead and beaten them to their spot! It wasn't a lonely spot for long! Without getting the needed solitude with His disciples, Jesus begins teaching and ultimately feeding the 5,000 men and their families who came to the little hillside to listen to Him. As soon as the meal was ended, Jesus insisted His disciples go ahead to the other side of the lake while He finished up and sent the crowd away. And then verse 46 tells us He went to the mountain to pray. He was alone. Praying to God, His Father.

The boat makes it to the middle of the lake while it is still *evening* (verse 47), and still Jesus is praying. The disciples don't make it much farther as a great wind comes up against them. At least 8 hours later the boat is *still* in the middle of the 8-mile wide lake. Oh how they must have cried out to God for help. Perhaps they even shouted to Jesus, hoping He would hear them. Where is He? Why does He remain silent? Why does He leave them in their struggle? Why does He stay along the shore instead of going out to rescue them? What in the world is He so busy doing? Why doesn't He just get out there and *rescue them from their trouble*? Remember what He was doing? That's right, praying. What or whom do you think He was praying about? I'll bet He was praying for them the whole time. Even though Jesus wasn't solving their crisis, He was interceding for them and *never* took His eye off their struggle. The beauty of that truth nearly moved me to tears. And Jesus does the same thing for us today. Sometimes it doesn't appear that God is answering us when we call out to Him, but even when your prayers for help are met with silence, be assured that Jesus is interceding for you and never takes His eye off you.

As you respond in worship to what God is showing you, please listen to "Healer" by Hillsong Live on the "This is Our God" album. Do you believe that nothing is impossible for Him? Do you know Him as the One who is more than enough for all of your needs? Will you trust God to be your healer? Will you ask God for a fresh touch today, trusting that He holds your world in His hands?

8

Rahab – My Identity is in My Past Baggage

Joshua 2:1-24, 6:15-25
Hebrews 11:31
James 2:25
Matthew 1:5

Anything that takes the place of God as our identity or the source of strength in our life has too strong of a hold on us. The women we have looked at so far have taught us about the danger of placing our identity in something other than God in order to feel *stronger and better* about ourselves. Looking to our career, our physical appearance, our children, or our sense of wealth and power as our source of strength and identity can be a real deterrent to building our life in Christ. But not all misplaced identities make us feel better about ourselves. Some make us feel defeated. Sometimes we cling to a self-image that stems from something in our past that weighs us down and from which we can't seem to find an escape. When we place our identity in our past baggage, our "I am" statements might look something like this: "I am insignificant." "I am unwanted." "I am used goods." "I am unloved." "I am abused." "I am rejected." "I am an adulteress." "I am a baby-killer." "I am worthless." These are some of the most difficult identity issues to confront because they typically involve painful situations and seasons from our past, some of which we may even have buried in our sub-conscious. Yet if we want to experience true freedom in Christ, we must address all of our mistaken identity issues, even the most painful ones.

The story of Rahab opens very dramatically in the book of Joshua as the children of Israel are finally beginning the conquest of their Promised Land. After wandering in the wilderness for 40 years, witnessing the death of everyone who came out of Egypt-including Moses-Joshua is instructed by God to cross the Jordan River and attack the city of Jericho. Prudently, Joshua sends two spies to search out the land and report back to him their observations. There is no doubt that Joshua would have chosen the two most godly men fitted for this task. Recall when Moses sent out the twelve spies in Numbers 13 and 14 to investigate the Promised Land and all but Joshua and Caleb said it was too dangerous and the enemy was too strong for them. God's anger at their lack of faith burned against them and as punishment He caused them to wander in the wilderness for 40 years—1 year for every day the spies had been in the land. Joshua was not about to let that happen again!

Why do you think godly men would choose to stay at the home of a prostitute? It doesn't seem a likely choice, does it? Perhaps they reviewed their lodging options and chose Rahab's home rather than an inn in town because her home was built into the wall and they could stealthily escape during the night after the city gates were locked. Perhaps she sought them out because she had already begun to believe in their God, and knowing He would destroy the city, she wanted to be offered protection. If she did seek them out, she would not have been the only one to have realized that they were spies from the children of Israel. Joshua 2:2 tells us that the king was even informed about the two spies being in Jericho. However she encountered them, certainly God had His hand in uniting Rahab with the spies as He had plans for her life that necessitated her breaking free from her old identity as Rahab, the harlot.

What are some of your own painful "I am" statements? Can you remember how they became a part of your identity? Please take some time to write about those experiences.

Paul tells us in Galatians 5:1 "It was for freedom that Christ set us free." God so desires for us to be free from the bondage of an old identity that He has washed us clean through the blood of His son, our Lord Jesus Christ. We can learn much from Rahab about stripping off an old, painful identity and knowing that we stand white as snow before a holy God.

SHE CONVERTS HEAD KNOWLEDGE TO HEART KNOWLEDGE

Rahab has learned much about this God of Israel, this God called Yahweh. She knows about the drying up of the Red Sea so the Israelites could cross on dry land, she knows about the cities that the Israelites had completely destroyed, and she knows their men are camped just on the other side of the Jordan. She and all her town with her are terrified of the God of Israel. But unlike the rest of the townspeople, Rahab does not just sit in a place of fear and dread, she chooses to think about what her response ought to be when faced with the awesome power of a God like Yahweh. And for each of us today, we have that same personal responsibility of deciding what we are going to do with what we have learned about this God. Rahab made her choice. She declares His Lordship over her life in Joshua 2:11 "for the LORD your God, He is God in heaven above and on earth beneath." In declaring Him "LORD" she uses His Hebrew name, Yahweh, and confesses Him LORD of her life.

Many people know a lot about God, many even fear Him, but that doesn't necessarily mean they *believe in* Him. King Abimelech, who greatly feared God when both Abraham and Isaac deceived him by lying about their wives, calls God "Lord" (not LORD-meaning Yahweh) in Genesis 20:4. This heathen king recognizes God's power and fears Him, but doesn't trust in Him. James 2:19 tells us that even the demons believe that there is one God; but that doesn't mean that they *trust in* God.

How about you? Have you ever declared Jesus as LORD of your life? Have you recognized your inherent sinfulness? Romans 3:23 declares the sad truth that "all have sinned and fall short of the glory of God." But God in His unending mercy and love for us has provided a way for us to become pure and spotless in His presence. He sent His son Jesus to take on our sinful nature, and to die on the cross for us and for our sins. In His resurrection He gives us His sinless nature, that we may stand pure before a holy God. It doesn't really matter how much you know about God, how wonderful you think He is, how good you try to be, or how often you make it to church. God's gift of salvation is not about how much *you* have done, it's about *what God has done for you* and whether or not you have accepted His gift to you. If you are not sure that you have asked God to be the Lord of your life and you want His power and presence to guide you, then come to God honestly and simply with a prayer of forgiveness. Nicky Gumbel, an Anglican pastor who is responsible for the creation and spread of the Alpha Course worldwide suggests a short prayer like this:

Sorry Lord for the sins I commit knowingly and unknowingly. I know my sins separate me from true relationship with You.
Thank you for sending Jesus to die on the cross to pay the price for my sins and to give me a new nature that is white as snow.
Please forgive my sins, fill me with Your Holy Spirit, and become the LORD of my life.

If you are making this commitment to Jesus Christ for the first time, or as a renewal of your faith, I encourage you to get connected into the body of believers as quickly as possible through a local church or Bible study group. Growth in our Christian faith happens best when we are in community with others, sharpening one another as "iron sharpens iron." (Proverbs 27:17)

We notice right away that Rahab is bold. She speaks boldly to the two spies about her faith in their God and that she will hide them in exchange for her family's protection. She also risks her life when she boldly lies to the king's messenger in order to protect the spies. When we are ready to cast off an old identity, we must come *boldly* to God and ask Him to heal us and give us a new identity. When we believe on Him for salvation, he sends His Holy Spirit to indwell and empower us so we are not struggling alone to overcome issues from our past. He is with us, helping us. We also must boldly declare to ourselves and to Satan that we have been transformed into the image of Christ and that our old identity has been washed away. We can confidently assert that when "any man is in Christ, he is a new creature; the old things passed away; behold, new things have come." (2 Corinthians 5:17)

Have you ever boldly asked God to remove the stigma of an identity you carry around with you? What happened as a result?

Sometimes we aren't even aware that we are defining ourselves by unhealthy identities. And other times we carry around old identities long after God has shown us that we need to lay them down. Why is this? *We can become so comfortable in an image we have of ourselves, even if it's a poor self-image, that we become unwilling to see ourselves in any other way.* Please reflect on that statement for a moment. The pattern we fall into every time we slide into self-condemnation is usually the same: We whisper the same words to our spirit. We arouse the same sensations of failure. We splash

around in the ugliness of it all. We know exactly what to do every step of
the way.

Is there a particular pattern of self-condemnation that you fall into again
and again? What do you say to yourself when you are in that place?

Is there any remedy for this type of self-defeat? Yes! Rahab shows us that
when we focus on the attributes and accomplishments of God rather than
on our own failures and weaknesses, we stand ready to strip off our old
identity and clothe ourselves anew. In every reference made of Rahab, she
is referred to as "Rahab, the harlot". Her name never appears without the
epithet, "harlot". It seems to define her. And yet, when she speaks to the
spies, she boldly declares her belief in their holy God without even once
calling to mind her own inadequacies. Nothing can change the fact that she
was a harlot, even as nothing can change the facts surrounding your past,
or perhaps even your broken present; but the question is, "will you let it
define you?" God's forgiveness through Christ is powerful enough to
cover even our greatest sins and the pain of an identity we need to cast off.

SHE WAS PREPARED

Have you noticed how quickly Rahab formulated an effective plan to help
the two spies? Not only does she hide them on her roof, and lets them
down from the roof in safety, but she instructs them to hide in the hills for
3 more days to be safe from their pursuers. This is her moment to begin to
break free, and she is well prepared!

Likewise, when we desire to break free from an old identity that enslaves
us, we need to do our homework and be prepared. We need a plan to

prevent our minds from constantly circling back to rest on our old identity. We are instructed to take every thought captive to the obedience of Christ (2 Corinthians 10:5). That means that when we catch our thoughts drifting into dangerous waters of self-condemnation, that we are to reel them right back to focus on something that is more pleasing to God.

Do you recognize when you are slipping into self-condemnation? If so, how can you practice taking those unhealthy thoughts captive to the obedience of Christ?

_____

Sharing our struggles with a believing friend can be very helpful in overcoming our issues of mistaken identity. Do you have one or two people in your life with whom you can honestly share your struggles?

_____

It is essential that we dig into God's word and claim His promises to us as we seek freedom in Him. Satan will do his best to keep you weighed down in the mire of your old identity. Don't let him! Just like Jesus, tell him "get behind me, Satan!" (Matthew 16:23) He has no authority in the lives of those who are following Christ.

God's promises to us about our identity in Him are plentiful. My son's friend, Ben Malcolmson, who is the Assistant to Pete Carroll, the Head Coach of the Seattle Seahawks, compiled a list of promises from God regarding our identity in Him. The list is so thorough and beautifully laid out that I wanted to share it with you here. He has given me permission to do so.

MY IDENTITY IN JESUS:

BELOVED "I have loved you with an everlasting love; I have drawn you with unfailing kindness." - Jeremiah 31:3

A CHILD OF GOD "See what great love the Father has lavished on us, that we should be called children of God! And that is what we are!" - 1 John 3:1

DELIGHTED IN "The Lord your God is with you, the Mighty Warrior who saves. He will take great delight in you; in his love he will no longer rebuke you, but will rejoice over you with singing."- Zephaniah 3:17

FORGIVEN "He himself bore our sins in his body on the cross, so that we might die to sins and live for righteousness; by his wounds you have been healed." - 1 Peter 2:24

WASHED CLEAN "Though your sins are like scarlet, they shall be as white as snow; though they are red as crimson, they shall be like wool." - Isaiah 1:18

FREE "It is for freedom that Christ has set us free. Stand firm, then, and do not let yourselves be burdened again by a yoke of slavery." - Galatians 5:1

A TEMPLE OF THE HOLY SPIRIT "Do you not know that your bodies are temples of the Holy Spirit, who is in you, whom you have received from God?"- 1 Corinthians 6:19

ADOPTED INTO GOD'S FAMILY "The Spirit you received brought about your adoption to sonship. And by him we cry, 'Abba, Father.'" - Romans 8:15

CO-HEIR WITH CHRIST "Now if we are children, then we are heirs — heirs of God and co-heirs with Christ." - Romans 8:17

RIGHTEOUS "For He made Him who knew no sin to be sin for us, that we might become the righteousness of God in Him."- 2 Corinthians 5:21

NEW "Therefore, if anyone is in Christ, he is a new creation: The old has gone, the new has come!" - 2 Corinthians 5:17

A SAINT "You were washed, you were sanctified, you were justified in the name of the Lord Jesus Christ and by the Spirit of our God." - 1 Corinthians 6:11

SET APART "You are a chosen race, a royal priesthood, a holy nation, a people for his own possession." - 1 Peter 2:9

AN AMBASSADOR OF CHRIST "We are therefore Christ's ambassadors, as though God were making his appeal through us." - 2 Corinthians 5:20

A CO-LABORER "For we are co-workers in God's service; you are God's field, God's building." - 1 Corinthians 3:9

A SWEET AROMA "For we are to God the pleasing aroma of Christ among those who are being saved and those who are perishing." - 2 Corinthians 2:15

NEVER ALONE "The Lord himself goes before you and will be with you; he will never leave you nor forsake you." - Deuteronomy 31:8

A MASTERPIECE "For we are God's masterpiece. He has created us anew in Christ Jesus, so we can do the good things he planned for us long ago." - Ephesians 2:10

WONDERFULLY MADE "I am fearfully and wonderfully made." - Psalm 139:14

BOLD "Since we have such a hope, we are very bold." - 2 Corinthians 3:12

HAVING GUARANTEED VICTORY "You have given me your shield of victory. Your right hand sustains me; you stoop down to make me great."- Psalm 18:35

HOLDING A SECURED FUTURE "'For I know the plans I have for you,' declares the Lord, 'plans to prosper you and not to harm you, plans to give you hope and a future.'" - Jeremiah 29:11

WHOLE IN CHRIST "In Christ you have been brought to fullness." - Colossians 2:10

All of these verses are words of truth for YOU! As a new creature in Christ, this is how God sees you. There's no mention of whatever word you commonly use to describe yourself. The old is gone; all things have become new.

Reread aloud the promises listed above, adding your name and "is" before each of the attributes listed in bold. How does that make you feel?

Which one(s) of these identities is the most meaningful to you?

SHE TAKES HER EYES OFF HERSELF AND THINKS OF OTHERS

Oftentimes we stay locked into an unhealthy identity because we refuse to take our minds off of ourselves and our own problems. Rahab's plea is for her entire family—her father, her mother, her brothers and sisters, and all who belong to them—to be spared from death in the ensuing battle. Did you notice that she doesn't actually even ask for *her own life* to be spared? When we are struggling with overcoming an identity from which God desires to free us, it is essential that we take our eyes off ourselves and focus on the needs of others.

When you are struggling with identifying yourself by the wrong "I am" statements, how difficult is it for you to look outside yourself and focus on others?

WHEN OTHERS WON'T LET YOU BE FREE

Rahab had faith in God, she was bold, she was prepared, and she took her eyes off herself to think of others; and yet, not even the two spies would let her enjoy her new identity in God.

Reread Joshua 2: 11, and verses 17-18. Immediately after Rahab's beautiful confession of faith, what do the two spies tell her she must do?

How humiliating that must have been for Rahab! Imagine the sting to Rahab of just having declared her faith in their God and her willingness to help them being met with, "here, just hang out your window this giant reminder that you are, after all, an immoral woman, and we will rescue you...even though you are a harlot." Even as purple is the color of royalty and white is the color of purity, scarlet has always been the color of immorality. Dating back to ancient times, scarlet has been the color associated with unchaste, immoral behavior. It is really no surprise that Nathaniel Hawthorne would choose scarlet as the color of the large letter "A" emblazoned across the chest of his main character Hester Prynne in The Scarlet Letter. Rahab, like Hester, must display the sign of her immorality.

Have you ever wondered where the scarlet cord came from? She must have already owned it, perhaps for advertising purposes. Perhaps the scarlet cord was hanging in her window when the spies arrived and that's how they thought she might have a room available. Perhaps she removed the cord when the spies arrived, and hid it along with them, as a sign of her new identity. Regardless of whether or not the cord was still in her window at the time of the spies' escape, they chose it as the identifying sign for Rahab's own future salvation. I can imagine Rahab longing for the spies to ask her to hang a *white* sheet out her window to identify her and her family at the time of the siege. But perhaps a white sheet or cord would have provoked too many questions from the same people who told the king that the spies were at her house. The scarlet cord would attract no extra attention and would in fact declare to the townsfolk that it's business as usual, at least for Rahab.

In Isaiah 1:18, the LORD declares: "Though your sins are as scarlet, they will be as white as snow; though they are red like crimson, they will be like wool." Imagine how much Rahab wanted that moment of cleansing to begin NOW!

How are you like Rahab? What sin do you struggle with again and again? What hurtful thing was done to you in your past that has given birth to debilitating "I am" statements that you put on auto-replay in your mind? Do you see yourself dressed in scarlet? Describe a new image of yourself where you are dressed in robes that are white as snow.

Have there been times in your life when you tried to break free from an unhealthy identity but you wouldn't let yourself because you continue to see yourself in that old identity? If so, please describe the situation.

Whatever your past, once you have come to Him for forgiveness God promises "there is therefore now no condemnation for those who are in Christ Jesus." (Romans 8:1) God longs to give you the identity of His Son, the Lord Jesus Christ. His work on Calvary washes away all of our past and allows us to clothe ourselves in Him. The second half of Galatians 5:1 that we looked at earlier is powerful indeed. "It was for freedom that Christ set us free; therefore keep standing firm *and do not be subject again to a yoke of slavery.*" When the enemy tries to keep you weighed down in the mire of an unhealthy self-image, it is crucial that you throw off that yoke of slavery by arming yourself with the promises of God and that you practice speaking those promises aloud as a reminder to yourself and as a rebuke to Satan.

Rahab longs to be freed from her past, but it seems even these godly men won't let her! The two spies, while grateful for her help, don't really see her for who she wants to be: a new creation in the LORD. She longs to be free from the yoke of slavery to her old identity as a harlot and be made new through the LORD.

Can you recall a time when you tried to break free from a damaging identity and people in your life wouldn't let go of the "old you"? Please describe the situation.

Sometimes even well meaning people in our life won't let us break free! Think about some of the people who have known you the longest. Do they continue to see you as you were (perhaps when you were a child) and not see who you are becoming? How about those who don't know you very well? Are they stuck in a "first impression" of you that doesn't accurately portray the "real" you? Notice how many times in these opening chapters of Joshua, Rahab is referred to as "Rahab the harlot". (See Joshua 2:1, 6:17, 6:22, and 6:25.) For crying out loud, how many other Rahabs are there in Jericho that are of interest to us in the book of Joshua? We all know who she is and what she has done; can't we just call her "Rahab" by this point? It seems she just can't escape her old identity.

Does your family insist on defining you by the image they have of you when you were a child? How does that keep you from experiencing God's freedom in your life?

In chapter 6 the siege on Jericho finally arrives. In a sweet moment of protection, it is the two spies themselves who go to Rahab's home to rescue her, her family, and all who belonged to them, before the city is totally destroyed and burned. They cared enough about her that they didn't want to risk anyone else going to rescue her and not being able to find her. But even after this tender gesture of kindness, the spies still identify Rahab by her old nature. They take her family and bring them back and place them "outside the camp of Israel." (6:23) Ouch. She has rescued Israel's spies, enabling them to attack her city, has professed her faith in and allegiance to their God, has expressed her desire to go with them, and still, they do not accept her new identity. Perhaps they don't fully believe that she will give up her old profession. Perhaps she is placed outside the camp because she is a foreigner. Or perhaps quite simply, she and all her family with her are considered unclean by Jewish law and until they have been purified, they simply must stay outside the camp.

It can take time for others to accept our new identity. Nevertheless, keep walking in faith with God while you wait for others to catch up. Eventually Rahab is accepted for who she is in God's eyes and is integrated into the people of Israel. In Joshua 6:25 we read "she has lived in the midst of Israel to this day." Not only does she find salvation, protection, and a home in Israel, she also finds love and security. Eventually she is able to fully cast off her past identity and she meets and marries a man named Salmon.

Regardless of how others may try to define you, it is essential that you learn to see yourself how God sees you. Take a moment to reread the "I am" statements that describe a person whose identity is found in Jesus Christ. This is your identity in Christ. But what about Rahab? She pre-dates Jesus. How did God really see her? In scripture, every verse about Rahab refers to her as "Rahab the harlot"—all the verses in Joshua, the verse in James, even the verse in Hebrews 11, the chapter referred to as the great "Hall of Faith". There is only one exception. In Matthew's genealogy of our Lord Jesus Christ, a surprising name appears as one of Jesus' ancestors. Rahab. Not "Rahab the harlot"; simply, Rahab. Finally she is epithet-free! Does it surprise you that Rahab is in the direct line of Jesus' ancestors? God is in the business of making all things new. Even Rahab. Even me. Even you. And when He recites the genealogy of His precious son Jesus, He's not about to describe one of Jesus' ancestors by her old identity. "Behold, (He is) making all things new!" (Revelation 21:5)

The last sound Rahab heard before her rescue from the city of Jericho and from her old identity was the sound of trumpets and shouting. It was her moment of leaving behind her old identity and clothing herself with an identity rooted in the LORD. Like Rahab, may this be our cry:

> "When He shall come with trumpet sound
> Oh may I then in Him be found,
> Dressed in His righteousness alone
> Faultless to stand before His throne."*

(*From the hymn "Solid Rock" by Edward Mote, 1834)

As you respond in worship to what God is showing you, please listen to "Amazing Grace (My Chains are Gone)" by Chris Tomlin on the "How Great is Our God" album. Thank God for His incomparable grace toward you. Will you accept in the depth of your being that your chains are gone and you have been set free from all of your past baggage? Let His mercy flood over your spirit today as you rest in who you are in Christ.

9

Breaking Free from an Ungodly Identity

1 Peter 5:8
2 Corinthians 10:3-5
Psalm 40:2-3
Ephesians 6:10-18

It has been quite a journey together, getting a glimpse into the lives of women God used in mighty ways to proclaim His love for us. Some of the women made great choices, and from them we get an example of how to live our lives to the glory of God. Other women did not make such wise choices, and from them we receive stern warnings about not putting anything before our love for God and our trust in Him. My prayer throughout this study has been that in getting to know these women of the Bible, that you would see some of your own areas of weakness where you have placed something else above your need for relationship with God. Did you identify any areas? Perhaps it's your need to excel at your career. Or is it your desire to be beautiful? Do you need your children to be the best at everything? Are you unable to admit when you are wrong? Do you yearn to be accepted, popular, and powerful? Or have health concerns or your own painful past experiences marked you with an identity you simply can't shake? When we place any of these things above our relationship with God, He calls that thing an idol. Not only is honoring an idol sin, but left unchecked, these idols become strongholds in our lives as they seep into every cell of our body until they become our identity.

Why do we cling to these idols, allowing them to become strongholds, or places where the enemy has gained access in our life? We perceive our unmet needs or desires as holes in our heart that we will continuously try to fill by our own efforts. Has your career stalled or never really gotten off the ground? You'll throw all of your energy and focus into your work to make it better. Is one or more of your children sick or living an unproductive life? You will fret and worry and do anything within your power to help them. Are you consumed by the size of your body or the emergence of new wrinkles every time you look in the mirror? Then you will invest in every product or program that promises to make you more beautiful or youthful. If you worry about being undervalued in your community then you will join every committee possible in order to expand your network of influence.

One of the questions I believe God is constantly asking us is, "Am *I* enough for you?" Our God is a jealous God. He will not share the throne of your heart with another idol. If we are very honest, many of us would say that God "plus" this one other thing is enough for us. But God is not very interested in the mathematics of God "plus" something else to fill the void. Remember, He calls Himself El-Shaddai, the all-sufficient one. Is He enough for you or have one or more of these idols come to haunt you so that it has become your singular focus? Listen in the stillness as God whispers to you, "Am *I* enough for you?"

We all have bumps, bruises, hardships and disappointments in life; it's part of our human experience. God longs to be with us in those challenges and to be our sufficiency. How do we walk through the trials and temptations of life, confident that His love for us is more than enough to fill the empty spaces?

ACKNOWLEDGE AND IDENTIFY

Before we can walk in the freedom God has for us by putting on His identity, we must acknowledge there's a hole in our heart and identify its source. Hopefully you have identified one or two strongholds in your life through this study so far. If you're still not sure you know where your strongholds are, then reflect on where your mind goes when it is in neutral. What are you longing for? Are you planning and strategizing something? What do you wake up thinking about in the middle of the night? Where your mind goes when you have time to be alone with your thoughts is a pretty good indicator of what's most important to you. I call that thing a "hole" in your heart because it's a need or desire that is screaming to be satisfied.

What are some of the "holes" in your heart where the enemy has been able to gain a foothold?

Some of us have been empty for so long that we don't even recognize how much we are trying to fill our lives with meaning and purpose aside from God. Furthermore, as we observe the secular world around us, nearly everyone is trying to fill their own empty spaces with anything they can find that will ease the pain. When we feel vulnerable, empty, or out of control in areas of importance to us, we will try to stuff ourselves with things we can control—like a rigorous exercise program, or an over-commitment to activities, or a rapid acquisition of material things. Ultimately none of this satisfies and so over time we will find ourselves needing more and more stuff to plug the holes in our heart. All of these small yet painful holes are simply symptoms of the bigger, more important unmet need, which is a fulfilling relationship with the living God.

God made man to be in relationship with Him and so when we are not in close fellowship with Him, we will be aware of a deep emptiness within us. Oh, of course we will identify it as an emptiness in our marriage, or in our career, or in our sense of beauty, health or popularity, but these are just symptoms of the much greater problem—our need to be in close relationship with God, and to allow His identity to become our own. When we pay attention to Him, we realize that God is wooing us into deeper and deeper places with Him, challenging us to consider how an increase in our trust in Him will produce a decrease in all of our other perceived needs. Only God alone can fill us in those deep, secret, empty places. When the God-sized hole is filled, our other perceived needs will lose their weightiness. The whisper grows stronger: "Am I *enough* for you?"

CONFESS AS SIN

Once I have acknowledged that my identity is not firmly rooted in Christ, and I have identified particular areas of difficulty or stronghold for me, I must confess these areas as sin. It is all too easy to call these areas "weaknesses" or "longings", and not identify them as "sin". It is sin when we place our identity in *anything* other than God.

Some people struggle with finding their identity solely in Christ because they want to add something to Christ's work on Calvary. They want to prove they were "good enough" or "worthy enough" of redeeming. And so they are perfectionists, working incessantly at self-improvement, hitting or exceeding the mark, locked into a cycle of performance anxiety. God tells us in the Old Testament and lest we forget it, repeats Himself in the New Testament, "There is no one who does good, not even one." (Psalm 53:3 and Romans 3:10) This truth doesn't seem to puzzle or surprise our holy God. It is in fact the reason why He sent Jesus to the cross. There is not one thing we can add to His work of redemption.

Others struggle with finding significance here on earth. They desperately need to know they have lived a life worthy of having been born. Their need for purpose and usefulness will propel them to always be accomplishing something—anything really—that helps justify their existence. God instructs us to "Cease striving (be still, let go, relax) and know that I am God." (Psalm 46: 10) He must be more important to us than our need to leave our mark on the world.

Still others simply need to be the best at everything they do, and if they're not, they don't even want to participate. The risk of trying and failing is too great for these folks. Perfection is the only option.

In which of these three areas do you struggle the most: needing to feel you are worthy of redeeming, needing to know you are useful and productive, or needing to be perfect? Can you identify the origins of this struggle?

Regardless of which of these groups you tend to find yourself in, the underlying problem is the same—PRIDE. Pride is my need to find my worth in myself rather than in God's love for me. When I am sitting on the throne of my life rather than allowing God to sit on the throne, it is all too easy for Satan to attack me with Pride's cousin—Fear. Fear is the anxiety that I won't measure up to the standard I (and sometimes others) have set for myself. When we are locked into habits of pride and fear, it is not only difficult to find our identity in Christ, it is also likely that our unmet needs will produce in us feelings of anxiety, depression, or self-pity. We must not dismiss these responses with a simple, "I'm not worried, I'm just feeling blue", or "I'm just doing this because I'm trying to provide for my family". We must name our behavior as sin and confess it. God promises us in 1

John 1:9 "If we confess our sins, He is faithful and righteous to forgive us our sins and to cleanse us from all unrighteousness."

How has the fear of not getting the things you most desire led to times of anxiety and self-pity in your own life?

―――――――――――――――――――――――――――――――――――――――

Write a short prayer of confession, asking God to forgive you for the things you have allowed to shape your identity because you have wanted these things more than God.

―――――――――――――――――――――――――――――――――――――――

RECOGNIZE THE SIGNS

When something other than Christ is on the throne of our life, we will be plagued either by fear that we won't get that thing we so desire, or by regret that we never got the object of our desire. Both of these scenarios expose us to attacks from the enemy. We learn from Peter that our enemy "the devil, prowls about like a roaring lion, seeking someone to devour. (1 Peter 5:8) This strong language speaks of Satan being constantly on the lookout for opportunities to attack us in order to achieve his number one goal—to make us doubt the Father's love for us.

How does the enemy attack us? Primarily through our thoughts. "But I'm a Christian," you say. "Satan can't inhabit my thoughts." That is correct. As a Christian, you are sealed with the Holy Spirit of God and Satan cannot penetrate that protection. But every one of us entertains all kinds of thoughts, all day, every day. Some thoughts are well-pleasing to God while others are outright lies and abhorrent to a holy God. When we do not cast out these self-deprecating, fear-driven, hopeless thoughts from our mind, we are giving Satan a foothold in our mind. One such thought, left unchecked, will beget another such thought, and so forth and so on until a habit of unhealthy, ungodly thinking has taken hold.

Paul refers to this as a stronghold, and in 2 Corinthians 10: 3-5, he instructs us on the enemy's role in the development of strongholds. In verse 5, Paul tells us specifically what these strongholds are: "logismous" or "reasonings" that take shape in the mind and are then worked out in life as action, and "hypsoma epairomenon" which are "human pretensions" or "arrogances" that have built fortresses with high towers aimed at repelling attacks by the knowledge of God.[12] Clearly, strongholds involve patterns of thought that are unhealthy, contrary to God's will, me-centric rather than God-centered, and that influence us to action (or willful inaction). These thought patterns can be so deeply entrenched that they leave us feeling hopeless and despairing of any chance of finding freedom.

How does the enemy work in us today? The same as he did in Eden—with words whispered deep into our spirits. If we are struggling with rejection, he doesn't *make* people reject us, but he does keep whispering to us that we are unworthy of being loved. He uses the same strategy on us today as he used on Eve. He manipulates words to suit his scheming needs. And like he did with Eve, Satan usually begins with a true statement, just to tempt us to keep listening. For example, if you are feeling lonely and on the "outside", you might think, "She doesn't like me as much as I like her." Or perhaps you are disappointed about being passed over for a recent promotion. You might think, "My boss thinks my colleague is better qualified than I am." Or if you are struggling with feeling unattractive, you might think, "I'm not as pretty as the woman next to me." All of these statements might be true, and that is why it is so difficult to recognize

Satan's tactics—because they usually do begin with a true statement. Once he has our attention with a truth, he twists it with a lie. And so, "she doesn't like me as much as I like her" becomes "I'm unlovable." "He's more qualified than I" becomes "I'm not good enough." And "I'm not as pretty as she is" becomes "I'm unlovely." All of these thoughts lead us to conclude, "I'll never measure up."

One Sunday a few years ago I was at church, worshipping in song, and my heart and mind were focused on God and His love for me. A friend was playing the piano that week as we sang, and at one moment I caught a glimpse of his profile and thought how much he and his son resembled one another. A sweet thought, right? The next thought to enter my mind was remembering that this son would be going off to camp that summer. Humm, where did that thought come from? And then out of nowhere (nowhere good, that is) the whispering thought came fast and furious, "Your son can't go to camp; he has diabetes." It hit me like a freight train. My breathing became shallow and tears began to well up in my eyes, as a great heaviness descended upon me. In no more than 5 seconds I went from dazzled in God's presence to despairing of all hope. How did this happen? I was worshipping. I was praising. While no one else was aware of what was happening to me, I was fighting a spiritual battle right there in church!

In God's sweet protection of me, we were singing "Blessed Be the Name of the Lord" as this was happening. Just as my despair was peaking we came to the refrain, "He gives and takes away, He gives and takes away. My heart will *choose* to say, blessed be the name of the Lord." As we sang that refrain over and over again, I knew that God and I needed to do some business together. This was a spiritual attack meant to separate me from the love of my Father. Would I give in? Would I allow the true statement, "my son can't go to camp" to morph into the lies that he wasn't loved by his heavenly Father, or that he wouldn't have a future and a hope in God? Would I believe Satan's lie that God loved me less than He loved someone

152

who didn't have major health issues in their family? It can be very tempting to believe the lies, but this time, thanks be to God, I chose to stand firm in the truth of who I am in Christ and who my son is in Christ. I recognized the signs of Satan's schemes. I had felt their familiar pattern before. I was able to rebuke him and feel the embrace of my Father's arms. By the time we reached the end of the song I was truly able to declare, "He gives and takes away; blessed be the name of the Lord!"

If we are observant, we will discover that, most often, these thoughts follow the same pattern every time—a physical manifestation of anxiety or sadness preceding the utterance of a phrase or two that we know very well but no one else knows that we repeat to ourselves frequently. Like a trigger on a trap, one thought can ensnare us in a spiritual battle of our identity. It's the same demeaning phrase that we have been repeating for years, for our internal ears only, and it may be accompanied by a change in heart rate, a nervous feeling, a welling-up of tears, or rapid breathing. Pay attention and train yourself to recognize when an attack is starting so that you can begin to fight against it. Learn Satan's whisper and his tactics so that like Christ, you can rebuke him and say, "Get behind me, Satan!"

What do your spiritual attacks look like? Please list as many of the "usual phrases" that come to your mind when Satan begins accusing you through thoughts. What physical feelings tend to accompany these thoughts? (If you have never considered that these episodes were spiritual attacks, you may not have paid close attention to the exact words and feelings that typically go together. Begin to pay more close attention so that you may be careful not to fall into Satan's trap.)

Please try to recount some situations when you fell into Satan's trap and repeated these accusatory phrases about yourself. What sets it off for you? Is it failure? Fear? Rejection? Inadequacy?

DON'T PUSH PLAY ON THE VOICE RECORDING IN YOUR HEAD

So you have acknowledged and identified areas where you have placed your identity in something other than Christ, you have confessed that as sin, and you are beginning to recognize the signs that a spiritual attack is happening. How do you stand firm and turn off the attack once it has begun? You must stop the voices inside your head that say you'll never be good enough, pretty enough, athletic enough, accepted enough, smart enough, successful enough, or respected enough. Only you can tell them to "STOP"! Only you can decide not to push PLAY on the voice recording in your mind that repeats the same lies over and over again. Everyone has a little soundtrack that they hear—yours is different from mine—but they all serve the same purpose: to accuse us before the King and to declare our unworthiness to a holy God.

Verbally rebuke Satan and deny his power over your thoughts, turning your thoughts to Christ instead. The passage we just read from 2 Corinthians 10 about strongholds ends in verse 5 with the secret to tearing down these strongholds in our mind: by "taking every thought captive to the obedience of Christ." We must willfully turn our thoughts from the lies of the enemy to the truth of our identity in Christ. It is not easy to take every thought captive to the obedience of Christ, especially not at first. But the more we practice the more we will be able to prevent these strongholds of the mind.

Why is it so hard to turn aside from the lies of the enemy? These aren't pleasant things we're listening to about ourselves, so why do we listen? Why do we believe them? Years ago, I heard the Bible teacher, Beth Moore, refer to these lies of the enemy as a mud pit that we willingly crawl into and slop around in. She draws that picture image from Psalm 40:2-3 "He lifted me out of the slimy pit, out of the mud and mire; he set my feet on a rock and gave me a firm place to stand." (NIV) Why would we choose to slop around in the mud pit of lies about ourselves? "It's a painful place," you say. "I would never *willingly* go into that place of despair."

Actually, it's quite easy to go into the pit and slosh around in the mud. We've been doing it for so long that we know exactly what to do when we get there. It's strangely comforting. These lies provoke feelings of self-pity, and self-pity is itself oddly comforting because its emphasis is all about me! When we are stuck in a pattern of self-pity our language is filled with "I am" statements: "I am stupid. I am horrible. I am unloved. I stink. I am unworthy." As much as we hate ourselves when we are in the mud pit, the comfort we derive from self-pity keeps us coming back for more.

Can you recount some occasions when you were stuck (even temporarily) in the pit of self-pity?

The alternative to wallowing in self-pity is actually much more difficult. To stop the chain of false thoughts that follows a true, painful statement such as: "I'm not as pretty as she is", "I'm not as talented as he is", or "I don't know the answer", and to respond inwardly: "but I'm loved by God," is like sailing in uncharted waters. We don't know what to do. We are not trained to deal with the painful truth; we would prefer to move right into the comfort of self-pity. And so, we often just stay in the pit where our thoughts and responses have been so strictly choreographed for years. Self-pity is really self-protection—we can't be found to be at fault if we have already declared that we are starting from a place of disadvantage. And so we crawl into the pit to protect ourselves.

Refer back to one of the situations you described earlier when you bought into Satan's trap of lies and got stuck in the pit of self-pity. Push REWIND and stop at your first painful thought. ("I can't believe I missed that ball." "How could I have done so poorly on that test?" "Why is my job so terrible?") Describe a different chain of thinking that would keep you focused on God's love for you and keep you out of the pit.

_____

Many Christians are quite convinced of God's love for them yet still have no victory in this area. God wants us to stop the chain of self-deprecation, self-pity, and fear and stand firm in His love for us. In his great chapter on the armor of God (Ephesians 6), Paul reminds us that when we are in a spiritual battle, God calls us to "stand firm" (verse 14). He doesn't ask us to advance or take new ground. But He doesn't want us to cave to our knees in insignificance either. He wants us to stand firm holding onto the shield of faith which will enable us "to extinguish all the flaming missiles of the evil one" that seek to tear us down (verse 16).

So you're not as popular as you wish you were. Stand firm in who you are in Christ. So your spouse has let you down...again. Stand firm in who you are in Christ. So you never felt the approval of your parents. Stand firm in who you are in Christ. So you may never enjoy the career success you expected you would. Stand firm in who you are in Christ. So you made a lot of mistakes in your past. Stand firm in who you are in Christ. When your identity is in Christ, even the painful truth can't destroy you. Let Him be enough for you.

PRAISE GOD

When we are in the thick of battle, in need of a quick escape, we need a battle cry to break our destructive thoughts and turn our mind to Christ. Like a general addressing his troops before battle, we must address the troops of our mind—our thoughts—with a call to action. The Three Musketeers would cry, "One for all and all for one", while Peter in "The Lion the Witch and the Wardrobe" shouted, "For Narnia…for Aslan!" Your own particular battle cry should be personal and effective at reminding you of who you are in Christ. Personally, I like to repeat, "I'm a child of the King. I'm a child of the King." I like the kingly language in this battle cry for it reminds me that someone is always on the throne of my heart. Will it be me or will it be the Lord? Other phrases such as, "I am fearfully and wonderfully made" or "He will never leave me" may also be helpful to you.

Give one or two examples of a fitting battle cry for you. Why is this helpful for you in particular?

Once we break the chain of negative thinking, it is essential that we immediately begin to praise Him. As we learned in the account of Leah, the Lord declares that He is enthroned on the praises of His people (Psalm 22:3), meaning that when we praise Him we give him authority to take up the throne of our life. There is no room for Satan's tricks when God is seated firmly on the throne of our heart because we are praising Him.

Set your eyes on Jesus and rest in the Father's love by repeating who you are in Christ. (Refer back to the long list of promises in Chapter 8 about your identity in Christ.) Clothe yourself with optimism in the assurance that He works all things out for His glory. Even our disappointments and failures. Even our shortcomings and regrets. Let Him fill you with a living hope for your future.

As you respond in worship to what God is showing you, please listen to "Break Every Chain" by Jesus Culture on the "Awakening – Live from Chicago" album. Do you believe that He is powerful enough to set you free? Will you let Him break every chain that keeps you from living a victorious life in Christ?

10

Staying Free in Christ's Identity

Colossians 3:1-4
Galatians 2:20
Romans 12:1-2
Philippians 2:5-8, 12-13
Colossians 2:6
Galatians 6:14-15

Breaking free from a stronghold that has formed our identity in anything other than Christ is an important step to growing in Christlikeness. In order to put on Christ's identity, something of ourselves, our ego, must necessarily diminish. In the language of the New Testament, we must "crucify" or "lay down" or "put off" the old self and its me-centric thoughts and ways. Only then can we put on Christ's identity. As I have said before, there is not room for both Christ and me to occupy the throne of my life.

When I was in high school and college, there was a popular chorus we used to sing at youth group taken straight from the King James Version of Colossians 3:1-3:

"If ye then be risen with Christ, seek those things which are above, where Christ sitteth on the right hand of God. Set your affection on things above, not on things on the earth. For ye are dead, and your life is hid with Christ in God."

That last phrase was repeated over and over as the refrain: "Ye are dead.

Ye are dead. Ye are dead and your life is hid with Christ in God." The tune was catchy and it was easy to find myself singing these words even when I wasn't with my youth group. But somehow the old English words like "ye" and "sitteth" made it easy to remove myself from any real sense of meaning to these words. What does it mean that I am dead? How can I be dead to myself and alive in Christ? That sounds like my life is not my own to live. What modern woman wants that as her legacy?

As I was writing the final chapters of this book my family was thrust headlong into a season of physical trials, most notable of which was my son's diagnosis with a rare disorder called POTS. Postural Orthostatic Tachycardia Syndrome is a disorder of the autonomic nervous system that causes my son's heart rate to double every time he goes from laying to sitting or standing. You can't imagine how tired he is every day as his heart races to pump blood around his young body. In addition to battling the fatigue, symptoms like brain fog and loss of appetite make my 17 year old son's life very challenging indeed.

Our usual rhythm together of carbohydrate counting, blood sugar testing, and insulin pump monitoring has suddenly been joined by daily rounds of new and curious medicines, reminders to drink copious amounts of liquid and eat sufficient amounts of salty snacks, efforts (translation: 'nagging') to ensure he get 11 hours of sleep a night, and coordination with teachers, tutors, and doctors. A common refrain I have used with friends and family who ask how I am doing is, "my life is not my own right now." It seems a fitting commentary on the state of things presently. There's no judgment, no anger, just a simple statement to say what I don't necessarily feel like saying. That a night of swinging blood sugars will cause enough sleep interruption to prevent him from going to school at all the following day. That some days I will have driven to and from the school 3 times before 1:00pm, leaving little time for me to tend to any work of my own. That tutors cancelling or quitting can upend an entire afternoon in a scramble to rearrange schedules. Some days it's frankly easier to simply say, "my life is not my own" and leave it at that.

As I was pondering the content of this final chapter and reflecting on the state of my family's situation, I reread a verse that, months earlier, I had identified as one that might be useful in this chapter. Galatians 2:20 (MSG) says "My ego is no longer central...The life you see me living is not 'mine', but it is lived by faith in the Son of God, who loved me and gave himself for me." *The life you see me living is not mine.* Wow! Now that's a sentiment I can understand and relate to! But what does it mean in the Christian context? *The life you see me living is not mine...ye are dead.*

What does self-denial look like for the believer? Does it mean I can no longer set goals for myself? Am I to have no drive, determination, or ambitions in life? Am I to become a doormat for others to walk all over? Not at all! At the most basic level, it means that I am no longer bound by the need to get my own way. I don't *need* to always be right, I don't *need* to be popular and powerful, I don't *need* to have the most successful children, I don't *need* to be healthy, wealthy, and wise. These things add nothing to my sense of who I am, and not having them doesn't ruin my day!

Dallas Willard, in his book *Renovation of the Heart* puts it this way: "Being dead to self is the condition where the mere fact that I do not get what I want does not surprise or offend me and has *no control* over me."[13] (emphasis mine) He goes on to say that to be truly Christ-like, I must lay down the burden of having my own way, which I can only do if I have a strong experience of God's all-sufficient presence in my life.[14]

Please reread that definition of "being dead to self". How often can you honestly say that not getting your way neither surprises you, nor offends you, and has absolutely no control over you? Certainly for many of us, not getting our own way has great control over our mood and even our actions. How many times do you find yourself enjoying a perfectly lovely

161

day when, Wham! something not to your liking happens, disrupting your tranquility, and suddenly your whole day seems ruined? It truly is a *burden*, as Willard said, constantly to need to have our own way.

The areas in which you fight most ardently to get your own way are most likely the areas in which you have the greatest identity strongholds. Are you constantly frustrated that your career is not progressing as you had wanted? You are probably basing your sense of worth in your job. Are you aware of every little time when you don't get your way in a discussion with your husband? You are probably striving to be the one with the most power in the relationship. Do you get angry when your children don't make the choices you are suggesting for them? You might be looking to your children's success to provide you with a sense of achievement.

Reflect back on the past week or two. Can you identify occasions when you didn't get your own way in something that was important to you? Perhaps you were misunderstood by someone who is close to you. Perhaps someone slighted you or a family member. How did it make you feel? Did you get angry or feel threatened?

Does it surprise you how greatly "not getting your way" offends and surprises you?

To really test how much not getting your own way has control over you, examine how you respond when you or someone you love one is treated unfairly (at least in your opinion!). When my oldest son was a senior in high school, he was hit by a drunk driver as he was driving home from a squash match. Even though his car was totaled, thankfully his only physical injuries were bruised ribs and a stiff neck and back. The following day his squash coach carried on with the scheduled challenge matches and my son had to play for a spot to see who would go to the Squash National Championships. It is no surprise that my son didn't fare very well in that match, less than 24 hours after being in a major car accident! What *was* surprising though, was the outrage and anger I felt at this second injustice against my son. I am embarrassed to say I found the coach's number, rang him up, and gave him a piece of my mind! How dare he make my son play for the final spot on the team when he had been at the hospital for tests only that morning? Once the coach calmed me down and allowed me to explain what had really happened to my son the night before, he scheduled a rematch for the following week and my son was able to earn his spot on the team. Long after the squash racquets had been put away for the season, I still had much to ponder about my own reaction to such a small incident in the scope of my son's life. I'm not saying the car accident was a small thing; but, not qualifying for the squash team was a small thing over the course of a lifetime. Why was I so angry at the thought of him not getting a spot on the team? Quite honestly, *I didn't get my way*, and it infuriated me. I had placed too much of my son's identity—and by extension, my own identity—in whether or not he qualified to go to the Squash Nationals.

How about you? Have you ever experienced something like I just described?

When disappointments or trouble or disasters come, and they will come, the question is, "does it destroy me?" If it does, there's an idol in the thing we lost. We are allowing it to form too much of our own identity. We can go 2-3 days, a few weeks if we're lucky, with no troubles. They are a part of life. As followers of Christ we need to examine our hearts in times of trouble and see how we respond. Can we lay the thing we want so badly at God's feet, declaring, "I can live without this. All I want and need is You."

How can you practice not letting these disappointments control you?

Keep testing yourself to evaluate where your affections lie. Difficult times have a way of revealing your true source of identity. We should always work hard at our goals, but our wins and losses, our successes and failures cannot control us to the point of defining who we are. In order for the Lord to bless us as much as He desires to, we must have the perspective that everything we have is His: our spouse, our children, our vocation, our wealth, our health, and so on. Will you trust Him with these things you hold so dear?

God's desire is for us to make an intentional transfer of our affections: to lay down our rights to control every detail of our lives, clothing ourselves with Christ's humility, and trusting that God's plan for us is better than any plan of our own making. How do we begin the process of self-denial and humbly laying down our rights before God? Paul gives us a practical lesson in the how-to's of self-denial in Romans 12:1-2:

"So here's what I want you to do, God helping you: Take your everyday, ordinary life—your sleeping, eating, going-to-work, and walking-around life—and place it before God as an offering. Embracing what God does for you is the best thing you can do for him. Don't become so well-adjusted to your culture that you fit into it without even thinking. Instead, fix your attention on God. You'll be changed from the inside out. Readily recognize what he wants from you, and quickly respond to it. Unlike the culture around you, always dragging you down to its level of immaturity, God brings the best out of you, develops well-formed maturity in you." (MSG)

The practical, contemporary voice of The Message makes it especially useful when we are drilling down to the practicalities of living a Christ centered life. Paul's exhortation to us is as simple, and as challenging, as starting each day with the question, "Lord, what do *you* want me to do with this day?" We all have plenty of ideas about what *we* want, but what if our focus shifted to wanting what God desires to accomplish through us?

What changes might you make to your attitudes or actions if you lived your life fully embracing the idea that your life is not your own but it is lived by faith in the Son of God, who loved you and gave Himself for you?

What is particularly scary to you about the idea of setting aside your own desires for your life?

Write a short prayer that you can use in the morning, dedicating your day to God, and that you can repeat throughout the day as you feel the need to recommit an aspect of your life to Him.

Often, we cling to a status we have created for ourselves—perhaps in terms of wealth or power or career—and if truth be told, we desire the advantages that level of status brings us more than we desire to be identified with Christ. Paul exhorts us in his letter to the church at Philippi to rethink things.

"Think of yourselves the way Christ Jesus thought of himself. He had equal status with God but didn't think so much of himself that he had to cling to the advantages of that status no matter what. Not at all. When the time came, he set aside the privileges of deity and took on the status of a slave, became *human*! Having become human, he stayed human. It was an incredibly humbling process. He didn't claim special privileges. Instead, he lived a selfless, obedient life and then died a selfless, obedient death— and the worst kind of death at that—a crucifixion." Philippians 2:5-8 (MSG)

Jesus invites us to follow his example of humility. Christ could have claimed the status of deity that was rightfully His, yet He put it aside out of obedience to and trust in God. There is no status that is rightfully ours, other than that of fallen man in need of a savior, and yet we desperately cling to statuses of success, beauty, wit, acceptance, popularity, and wealth as though our very lives depended on it. To be clothed in the identity of Christ is to put aside any desire for status and self-importance and to humble ourselves, living out Christ's life in us, in obedience to God. We will only be willing to do this and set aside our own desires and be identified with Christ when we really know Him and trust Him.

In order to live out Christ's life in us, we need to know what Christ is living for. Simply put, Christ was living to obey God and love others. That's a pretty good definition of self-denial! My life is to be lived in selfless obedience to God, transformed through the power of the Holy Spirit at work within me. Rather than living through my achievements, I must choose to live into my new identity in Christ. I am not only forgiven; I have been restored to a right relationship with God through Christ's work of reconciliation. When we are seeking to obey the Father and love others, it leaves us little time to be consumed and preoccupied by our own identity.

Paul continues in Philippians 2, encouraging us to "work out your salvation with fear and trembling; for it is God who is at work in you, both to will and to work for His good pleasure." (verses 12-13) The exhortation to *work out* this gift of salvation is coupled with the amazing promise that God is already, and for all time, at work *within* us. Transformation is not easy, and it does not happen overnight. Every day, and multiple times throughout the day, we must intentionally step off the throne of our lives, choosing to live a life of obedience to God and love for others. Paul says it well in his letter to the church at Colossae, "You received Christ Jesus, the Master; now *live* Him!" (Colossians 2:6, MSG)

The amazing thing about living in the identity of Christ is that it is far more liberating than living for myself. God's invitation to us is this: throw off the need to compete, to keep up, to be the best, and instead, rest in the grace of being loved and accepted apart from any personal merit. That is freedom! Paul describes this new way of living this way, "For my part, I am going to boast about nothing but the Cross of our Master, Jesus Christ. Because of that Cross, I have been crucified in relation to the world, set free

167

from the stifling atmosphere of pleasing others and fitting into the little patterns that they dictate. Can't you see the central issue in all this? It is not what you and I do...it is what *God* is doing, and he is creating something totally new, a free life!" Galatians 6:14-15 (MSG)

If you are very honest, how does your need to compete and be the best (perhaps even in terms of your Christian character and church work) influence the way you live?

Are you willing to throw that off and believe that you are loved and accepted apart from any personal merit?

The idea of denying myself and putting on Christ may seem unpleasant, hard, daunting even, until we really get to know this One whose life we are trying to live. The more we get to know Him, the more we come to realize that there truly is freedom when we live our lives for Christ. But how do we get to know Him in a deeper, more intimate way? How do we, in Paul's words, work out our salvation?

God does not leave us alone and helpless as we seek to deny ourselves and put on Christ. There are three things that we need to practice every day if we are to grow in our knowledge and love for Christ: Eat, Pray, Love. Okay, so I'm borrowing from the title of Elizabeth Gilbert's 2006 memoir of the same name, but hopefully the simplicity and familiarity of these three words will make them easy for us to remember! Eat—we must feast on the

Father's Word to us. Pray—we must spend time talking and listening to the Father. Love—we must receive the deep, deep love of the Father for us.

EAT

When I want to develop my love and trust in God and find my identity grounded in Him, I need to spend time getting to know Him intimately. He has given us His Word that we might feed on Him and learn from Him. Like the manna that fed the children of Israel during their wandering in the desert, we are to feed on God's word every day. Manna had to be gathered daily; it couldn't be gathered once for the entire week. Likewise, we must dig into the Word daily to receive from God; once a week at church is not enough.

So often we approach our time with God as though it were a frivolous add-on to our list of necessary things we have to do in a day. When we treat Him like this, we never end up with enough time to meet with Him. Let's face it, there's never enough time in a day to accomplish all the necessary business, so we must start with the vital things. Our professional work, our domestic work, our work as caregivers are all necessary things. Spending time with God is vital. There are many ways we can spend time in His Word. We can focus on one book of scripture at a time, with or without a supplemental study guide. We can vary our reading from the books of the Gospels, to the Epistles, to the books of history, to an extended period of time delving into the Psalms. We can read the scriptures assigned to the liturgical calendar or a One-Year Bible, getting readings from the Old and New Testaments, the Psalms and Proverbs. We can also pick up a topical book, using scripture as a supplement to our reading. Or, we can focus in on one or two verses at a time and meditate on their truth. There is no one way to spend time in God's word; but it is essential that we put time with Him first. Feasting on His Word gives us the fuel to serve Him.

Jesus quotes Deuteronomy 8:3 when He tells us that "man shall not live on bread alone, but on every word that proceeds out of the mouth of God." (Matthew 4:4) He has lavishly given us His Word to feed us. It is vital that we develop a habit of reading the word of God, and that what begins as discipline becomes the most desired and essential thing we do in our day. No matter the issue that you are facing, God has a word for you. Come to the banquet that He has set before you and feast on Him!

Describe your current habit (or lack of habit!) of reading the Word. At this particular stage of your life, when is the best time of day to feast on His word to you?

What could you do to keep your Bible time fresh so that it is the most essential, non-negotiable part of your day?

PRAY

Considering how important prayer is to our spiritual development, it is surprising how uncomfortable even long-time Christians can be at practicing the spiritual discipline of prayer. Prayer is meant to draw us into the presence of God, to a place of deep communion with Him. A particularly good time for prayer is after our time reading the Word, because we have already come to God asking Him to speak to us. But not all prayer consists of long blocks of time praying through a prayer list. A rich prayer life will also include frequent times of "spontaneous conversation" with God as we share with Him the deepest burdens, anxieties, and joys on our heart.

We cannot break free from an ungodly identity without prayer. Every step we take to break free from an identity that is not Christ's requires us to be in conversation with God. As soon as we recognize a hole in our heart, an unmet need, a sense of wounded pride, we must go immediately to God in prayer, giving Him permission to search our hearts and help us understand our pain. Don't wait until it's time for an "official" prayer time—pray immediately! When a feeling of sadness overtakes you, or you are tempted to push "Play" on that voice recording, pray immediately, asking God for wisdom and understanding.

Prayer also gives us an opportunity to hear from God. This is, I believe, the most difficult part about prayer. It's already a leap of faith to talk to a God whom you cannot see, but how do you *listen* to a God whom you cannot see? How do we know when we are "just sitting still" and when we are "listening to God"? In a world of distractions it is very difficult to sit and be still and listen for God's voice. But it is perhaps the most important thing we can do if we want to know the love of the Father for us. In his beautiful book, *Life of the Beloved*, Henri Nouwen has this to say about listening as we come to prayer:

"...I realize that, although I have a tendency to say many things to God, the real "work" of prayer is to become silent and listen to the voice that says good things about me...It is not easy to enter into the silence and reach beyond the many boisterous and demanding voices of our world and to discover there the small intimate voice saying: 'You are my Beloved Child, on you my favor rests.' Still, if we dare to embrace our solitude and befriend our silence, we will come to know that voice."[15]

To grow in our prayer life, we must learn to be still and listen. We won't hear an audible voice, but we will begin to recognize His voice speaking to our spirit. Like learning to deny ourselves or spending time in the Word, it takes practice to develop our listening skills. We need never fear what He might say to us during those times of listening. He loves us perfectly and He tells us that perfect love casts out fear. (1 John 4:18) Sometimes in the quiet, He will reveal to you something He needs to teach you; but don't be afraid of this voice. He always convicts to correct, not to condemn. Sometimes in the quiet, He will reveal to you something of His great love for you. This kind of blessing can only come when we have quieted our loud hearts long enough to receive a touch from God.

Describe your typical prayer times. Do you take time to listen to God? Do you also have times of "spontaneous conversation" with God throughout the day?

_____

When we aren't accustomed to quiet stretches of time spent listening to God, it can feel awkward at first. Begin with smaller amounts of time and build this up as you get more comfortable and when have more time available. When could you fit in a time of listening to God and how might you practice this?

_____

LOVE

The real story of the Bible, the one that flows through all 66 books of the Old and New Testaments, is a love story, where God is the Lover and we are the Beloved. The narrative opens in Genesis with the Creator yearning for intimate fellowship with His Beloved, and culminates in Revelation with the long-anticipated wedding feast of the Lover and the Beloved. On the pages in between, the invitation is repeated over and over again: receive the deep, deep love of the Father for you.

If we really understood and believed the Father's immense love for us, the things we currently desire—popularity, wealth, success, beauty, etc.— would pale by comparison. If we truly knew and trusted this God of the universe, we would realize that our deepest longings are fulfilled in Him alone. If I could fully grasp that His love for me has nothing whatever to do with my own attempts at demonstrating my worthiness, I could finally be set free from the need to prove my own worth.

But our world is filled with voices that are all too quick to give the defining verdict, "You don't measure up." Receiving too many of these messages will quickly drown out the verdict of the Father, "You are my Beloved; in you I am well pleased." In *Life of the Beloved*, Nouwen explains why it is so difficult for us to believe in the Father's great love for us.

"These negative voices are so loud and so persistent that it is easy to believe them. That's the great trap. It is the trap of self-rejection. Over the years, I have come to realize that the greatest trap in our life is not success, popularity, or power, but self-rejection. Success, popularity, and power can, indeed, present a great temptation, but their seductive quality often comes from the way they are part of the much larger temptation to self-rejection. When we have come to believe in the voices that call us worthless and unlovable, then success, popularity, and power are easily perceived as attractive solutions. The real trap, however, is self-rejection. I am constantly surprised at how quickly I give in to this temptation. As soon as someone accuses me or criticizes me, as soon as I am rejected, left alone, or abandoned, I find myself thinking: "Well, that proves once again that I am a nobody." Instead of taking a critical look at the circumstances or trying to understand my own and others' limitations, I tend to blame myself—not just for what I did, but for who I am. My dark side says: 'I am no good...I deserve to be pushed aside, forgotten, rejected, and abandoned.'

Maybe you think that you are more tempted by arrogance than by self-rejection. But isn't arrogance, in fact, the other side of self-rejection? Isn't arrogance putting yourself on a pedestal to avoid being seen as you see yourself? Isn't arrogance, in the final analysis, just another way of dealing with the feelings of worthlessness?...Self-rejection is the greatest enemy of the spiritual life because it contradicts the sacred voice that calls us the "Beloved." Being the Beloved expresses the core truth of our existence."[16]

How does it make you feel, knowing that you are the Beloved of God?

How does understanding God's deep love for you help you to re-think some of the identity issues you struggle with holding onto?

God's call to us is not one of *self-rejection* but one of *surrender*. He says to us, "Cease striving and know that I am God." (Psalm 46:10) "Come to me all who are weary and heavy-laden and I will give you rest." (Matthew 11:28) Isn't it time to stop striving under the burden of maintaining an identity based on anything other than God? Isn't it time to surrender every part of you to the living God?

We will only surrender to one who is worthy of our surrender and to whom it is safe to surrender. Surrender is only really "safe" when we give ourselves to one who loves us more than we could ever imagine. God's love for you is like that. It is immense. It never has to be earned and it can never be lost. He loved you while you were still His enemy, lost in your sin and separated from Him. His love for you will always out-measure your love for Him. He would give the whole world for you; in fact, He gave His own Son for you, because He loves you that completely.

When we begin to grasp the Father's deep love for us, then we can live securely in the knowledge of who we are in Christ. True understanding of our identity in Christ frees us up to be less concerned with how others perceive us—which is living in our old identity—and more focused on how we can love others. This is the love of Christ living in us: obeying the Father and loving others.

As we experience the love of the Father, He will make us more like Him. Living each day firmly convinced of our identity as a child of God enables us to love others like God loves us. Knowing that I am a child of the king reminds me that it is His kingdom for which I am living, not my own. It is my joy and honor to bring *Him* glory. I no longer live for myself but for Him.

Listen to Him whisper: "Lay down your need to be identified by anything other than Me. Imitate Me by obeying Me, denying yourself, and loving others. Lean on Me for your source of strength rather than trying to prove your own worth by what you can do or who you think you are. I have loved you with an everlasting love. You are my Beloved; in you I am well-pleased."

As you respond in worship to what God is showing you, please listen to "Rooftops" by Jesus Culture on the "Come Away (Live)" album. As you seek to stay free and accept His boundless love for you, will you feast on Him today? Go deep with Him in prayer. Stand before Him with your arms wide open and receive His immeasurable love for you. Will you place everything that you are into His loving hands and tell Him, "I am yours"?

[1] *Webster's New Collegiate Dictionary* (Springfield, MA: G & C Merriam Co,

[2] JA Motyer, *The New International Dictionary of the Bible* (Grand Rapids: Zondervan, 1987), "Acrostic", 12.

[3] Confucius, *Sayings of Confucius.*

[4] Leo Tolstoy, *The Kreutzer Sonata,* translation by Louise and Aylmer Maude (Tolstoy Library OnLine, first published 1889), Chapter V.

[5] Clinton E. Arnold, *Zondervan Illustrated Bible Backgrounds Commentary: Volume 2, John, Acts* (Grand Rapids: Zondervan, 2002), 251.

[6] Arnold, *Zondervan Illustrated Bible Backgrounds Commentary: Volume 2, John, Acts,* 251.

[7] Stephen Schwartz, *Popular* from the musical *Wicked,* 2003)

[8] Arnold, *Zondervan Illustrated Bible Backgrounds Commentary: Volume 2, John, Acts,* 251.

[9] "Women and the Law of Moses", http://www.christianleadershipcenter.org/women6.htm.

[10] M. Tichi, "The Cycle of Women and the Niddah", http://www.yahshammahlove.sabbatarian.com/content/Niddah.html.

[11] "Redeem", *The King James Bible* Page, http://www.King James Bible Page.com—av1611.com/kjbp/kjv-dictionary/redeem.

[12] "Spiritual Weaponry", http://www.biblegateway.com/resources/ivp-nt/Spiritual-Weaponry.

[13] Dallas Willard, *The Divine Conspiracy,* (New York: Harper Collins, 1998), 71.

[14] Willard, *The Divine* Conspiracy, 75.

[15] Henri Nouwen, *Life of the Beloved*, (New York: The Crossroad Publishing Company, 1992), 75-76, 77.

[16] Nouwen, *Life of the Beloved*, 31-32,33.

Made in the USA
Monee, IL
28 February 2020